DROP DEAD GORGEOUS

Tome of Memories

Mary Eicher

Published by Mary Eicher

Production Team
Trish Beaulieu, Literary Agent, book division manager, and editor;
Nancy Ratkiewich, book production, njr productions,
Rachael Eicher-Graziani, cover designer, and
Audio Engineer, XV Podcasters.

For general information on other products and services, please visit the website: www. officialmaryeicher.com

ISBN: 979-8-9910310-2-8 Paperback
ISBN: 979-8-9910310-0-4 eBook
ISBN: 979-8-9910310-1-1 Audiobook

Printed in the United States of America

Gwyn is having a hell of a day. Sure, her image in the mirror is gorgeous, but she cannot remember her name and has no idea who or what she is. The past is a blank, and her present is full of questions. As she moves into the future, Gwyn finds danger and absurdity abound.

She discovers she is a grim reaper and humanity is in desperate need of her services. The dead refuse to rest, and the living are oblivious to a looming catastrophe as the barrier between realms begins to disassemble.

Gwyn's major source of guidance is an ancient tome containing the memoirs of reapers from eons past. An enigmatic figure offers insight and protection. Gwyn wonders if the charmer is the savior he claims. Or does the darkly alluring Mr. Black harbor the key to the memories that have been stripped from her?

Gwyn searches for answers while also trying to understand the amusing and illogical behaviors of the humans she reaps. Prepare to be entertained by a sarcastic take on destiny and the human condition where nothing is quite what it seems.

CHAPTER ONE

Without a Lantern, Looking for Myself

Stardust swirls in the incomprehensible universe. Dispassionate particles subject only to the gentle grip of gravity. The cosmic wind sweeps them into spirals and galaxies where mindless atoms become molecules, which in turn become elements, and life emerges. I am begun.

It happened just before dawn. Pale light was slipping through the window blinds making gray stripes along a black wall. All else was shape and shadow, dark forms at once familiar yet unremembered. I lay in bed a while, listening to rain tap against the window, wondering at the blackness in my head where memories belonged. I had knowledge of the world, of species and science, stark facts about the realm surrounding me. But none of these revealed who I was or what my purpose might be. *How could I have come to this*, I wondered, tossing aside the blanket at last and getting to my feet.

The room began to brighten; yellow bands of sunlight illuminated the space around me. I filled my lungs with cool, damp air and saw my reflection in a nearby mirror. She was a stranger, thin and well-formed with a pale complexion, blonde hair curled to her shoulders and blue eyes wide with questions. Given her physical form, I assumed myself to be a young human female. It was the first of the many incorrect assumptions I am given to make.

The air was cool, so, I wrapped myself in a black cloak and selected a pair of fur lined boots. The cloak enclosed me, neck to feet, in a comfortable cocoon. It had long sleeves and numerous pockets within and without. It suited me. Even my reflection approved.

The living room had furniture gathered into a seating area and an assortment of storage devices running along the back wall. I meandered through, seeking clues about the one, presumably me, who lived there. Lingering at a desk in the corner, I searched the files and cubbies, not finding a scrap of paper. No mail, no documents, nothing to suggest my identity.

I ran my fingers along a row of books, and a line from Emily Dickinson came to mind. "Without a lantern looking for myself." That was me in spades. All brawn and no background to ruin a cliché. I passed my hand along a row of book spines. Each book I touched filled my thoughts with a saying or aphorism. Einstein said, "The true sign of intelligence is not knowledge but imagination." Whoever the hell I was, I evidently had the social life of a well-read hermit.

My inspection of the apartment proved futile, I spent a while at a window observing people in the street below dashing through the now heavy rain. I was jealous of the purposefulness that propelled them as they scurried along. I felt no such urgency nor any clarity regarding my own situation. I decided to see if spending time among them would establish a deeper connection. Possibly, one of them might recognize me, I reasoned and provided the answers that my empty memory could not.

I made my way out of the apartment and down the stairs to the building's exit. The rain had become a torrent, and I paused at the door to pull the cloak hood over my head before stepping out into the tide of humanity trudging through the downpour. I found the sensation of rain on my face pleasant as I studied the buildings lining either side of an asphalt road. Most were single-story boxes no bigger than my apartment; all were decorated in bright swathes of graffiti promoting local gangs. Several of the buildings like mine rose to three stories, silent sentinels of a more prosperous era.

Vehicles whisked by sending sprays of water onto the sidewalk, dousing people, already soaked, who nonetheless jumped to avoid the little waves. The irritated pedestrians bumped into each other, apologized, or cursed, then proceeded on their way. Huddling closer to the store fronts, I was spared the pinball effect they caused. I was, in fact, ignored. No one made eye contact with me or responded to my greetings. I could hear them speaking with each other despite the sound of vehicles, footfalls, and voices struggling over each other in a nerve-jarring cacophony. I absorbed it all searching for the feeling I belonged.

After several blocks, I passed a restaurant where people sat at tables consuming food and drink. The hollow feeling in my gut protested, and I decided to join them. Before I could go in, a nearby disturbance caught my attention. People were shouting and running toward a person lying on the pavement. Beside the stricken figure stood a fellow donned in a cloak identical to mine. He waved at me and smiled. His reaction took my breath away, and the inner emptiness gave way to a burst of hope.

The dense crowd prevented me from getting closer. I called out just as a ghostly form rose from the body on the pavement, and my acknowledger turned away. He gathered the floating form, then donned his hood. Immediately, they disappeared. I think I wanted to cry; so disappointing was the loss. Possibly, I did. It was impossible to tell in the rain, and I was not certain I possessed the ability to cry like some of the onlookers.

Lowering my hood, I wiped the water from my eyes and made my way back to the eatery. A waitress in a cheerful pink apron greeted me and offered to show me to a table. She mumbled about the miserable weather that was somehow hurting business and walked me to a free place in the center of the room. She asked to take my dripping cloak, which I unclasped and began to remove. The room erupted into shouts and laughter. Evidently, one was expected to wear garments beneath a cloak.

I redonned my singular garment but was escorted from the premises anyway. I pondered the behaviors I had seen as I headed back to the quiet safety of my apartment. Unlocking the front door, I dropped into a chair and reevaluated my earlier assumption. I was not a human. I was not even versed in humans. I was whatever the cloaked fellow who had claimed the ethereal form was. And I was glad of it.

A package addressed to 'Occupant' was delivered bright and early the next morning. In it were a laptop, a printer, and a cell phone. I logged on as an *occupant* just for fun, and to my amazement, it worked. The password was, less surprisingly, *password*. In response, I was presented with a screen full of possibilities. Maybe I was not meant to learn who I was, I thought. Maybe I could invent whom I wanted to be.

I selected the name . . . Gwyn. The surname, Reaper, was added automatically. I liked the name—Gwyn Reaper—it made me feel real. I browsed the other information on the PC and learned more about a communication device embedded beneath the skin of my left wrist. It was called a plaz; and there were other tools available to me. Tools for use in a function I had observed the cloaked man perform. I was a reaper of human souls. Mark Twain said, "The most important two days in your life are the day you are born and the day you find out why." I pulled my hand away from the bookcase and chuckled. *I have got to stop fondling those damn books!*

Next, I chose a profession for what would be my public persona. An occupation that would discourage human attachment and give me enough flexibility to manage reapings likely to occur at any time. Moments later, I was Gwyn Reaper, IRS agent with an office address and a phone number embossed on the business cards issuing from the printer.

Within an hour, I had a bank account generously loaded with ample funds, an unlimited credit card, a resume that included a degree in finance, and the pink slip for a seven-year-old Chevy. The empty cubbyholes in what was supposed to be my memory remained blank, but that no longer mattered. I had an identity I felt comfortable with, at least the day job part, and a purpose. Mr. Twain would have undoubtedly approved.

Just before logging off, my email displayed a message that read:

GWYN, LET'S HAVE DINNER SOON. ELLY

News travels fast, I noted and typed in SURE then clicked reply.

Putting aside the computer I went to the kitchen to make a sandwich. There was a lot to chew on. What would it be like to reap a soul? Where is the portal? Who the hell is Elly?

I used the rest of the day, appropriately dressed, spending some of my new-found fortune and familiarizing myself with the establishments near my apartment. There were mainly bars, eateries, and liquor stores, but occasionally something unique caught my eye. Like the reptile store on Adams. I stopped to observe the five-foot Eastern Indigo in the window. He lifted his head to stare right back at me. He was sleek, dark gray in color with a dash of orange low on his head. There was an intelligence in his eyes and an expressed curiosity.

I returned to my apartment with my new friend, Felix, and all the accoutrements he would need. A box large enough to contain a snake of his size, filler and logs to construct a privacy area for him, assorted nutrients, and a month's supply of frozen mice to be thawed one at a time.

Felix inspected every inch of the apartment while I assembled his cage. When it was completed, he slithered over for a look and gave me a thumbs up using his tail for the non-existent digit. He settled into a lazy coil for the night while I settled on my bed with a book and hoped leaving the bedroom light on would not disturb his sleep. It did not disturb mine. Just after midnight, my plaz illuminated my wrist with a message stating name, place, and time:

AUGUST DANBRIDGE, 56, NUMEN ALLEY 12:45 AM

My body reacted exactly as programmed. I grabbed my cloak and my, seemingly self-directed, feet hastened me to the door. I found Mr. Danbridge behind one of the tawdrier drinking rooms lining the streets. A man in his middle fifties was slouched against a battered trash bin. He was filthy and there was a bullet hole in his forehead. Beside the body stood a spirit version of the guy impatiently tapping a translucent foot.

""Took you long enough!" the spirit spat out.

"Sorry, traffic," I lied, visions of the young reaper I had seen earlier popping into my head. He had touched the spirit, then disappeared. I reached out to grab the guy's arm.

"What are you doing?" Danbridge avoided my grasp. "Aren't you supposed to fix my body or something?"

"There's no fixing that," I stated firmly pointing, at the bullet hole.

"Well, hell, then," he crossed his arms. "So, you're saying I'm . . . dead."

I nodded. "Evidently. Come on. Let's get you where you're going."

Danbridge seemed to sober up a bit. "Ah, well, you don't happen to know where that is, do ya? I mean, what happens to a fellow like me?"

"All I know is I'm to take you to a portal," I told him rechecking the new coordinates illuminated on my wrist. I saw no point in telling him I was flying as blind as he was. It was a first for us both. He quivered nervously, an odd sight considering he was essentially transparent and commenced to pace in a sort of jerky back-and-forth swooshing motion. Then he began to sweat which added another distortion to the ethereal entity. It was not at all what I had assumed ghostly behavior would be.

I waited while he gathered himself, clearly apprehensive about his circumstance.

"Come on," I said, pulling on my hood while I took his hand and got a jolt of why he was so reluctant. His had been a life spent evading consequences, an unsuccessful life even in Danbridge's own estimation. Yet there had been moments when he had tried to best the demons of his own selfishness. Within moments we arrived at a rocky structure, and an iron gate swung open. As I watched him enter the portal, I found myself hoping the man's finer moments would be enough to sustain him through whatever awaited.

I made it home by the witching hour, went into the bedroom, and changed into a pair of men's boxer shorts topped with a Wonder Woman-themed t-shirt, my preferred sleep attire. Looking in the mirror, I fluffed the hair of the bedraggled image, staring back at me, then made my way into the kitchen. I was not hungry, but a bit of hot chocolate sounded appealing. I brushed the counter clutter to the side and tossed a cup of water into the microwave to heat while I found the packet I needed.

Felix slithered across the counter and reared up for me to pat him on the head.

"Hello, ole boy. Sorry, I abandoned you on your first sleepover. Let me make it up to you with a late-night snack." I sorted an item out of the fridge, tapped the mouse corpse on the counter, and dangled it by the tail for my pet. Felix secured the meal with a quick strike and settled back to consume it.

Chocolate in hand, I meandered into the living area, called up the huge television screen illuminating a muted version of local news. There were the usual traffic snarls, sports outcomes, and the forecast for more rain in the morning. A typical gloomy spring weekend loomed before me, and I did not mind a bit. In fact, the idea of putzing around, alone with my thoughts was appealing.

My attention wandered to the numerous posters framed and mounted on the plain white walls of my living area. Each poster was a drawing of a medieval grim reaper creating a gallery of hooded, skeletal figures with huge scythes and sardonic grins. A family album of sorts, though strictly from the human point of view. According to the information I had reviewed on the computer, actual reapers are the antithesis of the medieval drawings. Most reapers would be considered gorgeous by human standards with our planed faces illuminated by pale eyes. Our trim, athletic bodies varying only in height and gender. Reapers possess a timeless physical perfection blended with an aloof, dispassionate nature.

Felix settled next to me. Snakes are excellent pets. They are sleek, predictable, and emotionless; in some ways more like reapers than humans are. Like reapers, snakes are maligned as evil. Their venom dispatches humans to the afterworld, culling the weak and unwary. Patient and secretive, Felix is a perfect companion, requiring little and judging not at all.

I turned off the TV and reclined on the couch to catch a few hours of sleep. Pulling a blanket over me, I checked the communication device embedded in my wrist for messages. Finding none, I let sleep take me to a place where oblivion resides aside dreams. I choose dreams having had more than enough of the oblivion of amnesia.

Those early days were a continuum of firsts. I found the IRS building and my rather spacious office on the second floor. Liz, my administrative assistant, was a treasure in wolves clothing. I was, to all the clients we processed, merely a wolf. I learned humans are obsessed with money. I think they must dream of rolling in it, naked, drinking champagne, while gold coins shower down upon them. Asking them to part with their money is a kind of murder much worse than being boiled in oil. Especially if it is the government making the demand. Between reaping the newly dead and garnishing wages, I prefer the less emotional activity of reaping.

I took a long walks in the forests some days and drove to the ocean on others. I found both exceedingly pleasant. This planet has a compelling beauty which as far as I could tell humans are largely oblivious to. They cluster in towns and cities making sure to strip away any remnant of the flora and fauna to which they deem themselves superior. They live atop each other, amid chaos, unable to conceive of a moment of solitude, as far as I can tell. They call it civilization. I call it madness.

Not that I fail to grasp the meaning of being lonely. So many of them are and yet they take great pains to conceal their true selves from each other. Their natures are revealed to me with a simple touch. And humans ignore their instincts while distancing themselves from the realities they choose not to accept.

I do not dislike humans. They are for the most part well-meaning and often sympathetic. I merely find them amusing. They are as oblivious to the richness of the universe as I am unable to fathom the systems I am bound to. Knowing what to do is not as pleasing as knowing why I must do it.

I spent long hours reading the books accumulated in my apartment. Sampling philosophy, metaphysics and religious dogmas provided insight into the human condition. But I found no answers to satisfy me.

Within weeks I had settled into a routine. My apartment had become a monument to chaos theory. There were stacks of IRS files in each of the three rooms. Discarded clothing graced the backs of furniture and empty food containers seemed to congregate on horizontal surfaces where I suspected they were procreating. Nothing was in its proper place assuming any item had ever had one. Yet there was an elegance to the space. A resistance to the superiority of order; a refusal to acquiesce to rules. Virtues, according to Elly, who turned out to be my self-appointed mentor, I possess in abundance.

I came home one evening to find Felix hissing at me and followed him into the bedroom. Lifting him into my arms, I sensed his distress. The dust bothered him. And there was plenty of dust. I busied myself vacuuming and unburdening surfaces so they could be wiped taking special care of the area around Felix's cage and my nearby bed. Which is how I found the book.

More than just a book, what I discovered under my bed was an ancient tome bound in decorated leather and filled with hundreds of hand written parchment pages. It was like finding the past with a big red bow on it. There hundreds of first-hand chronicles of reapings spanning thousands of years. They were not my memories, but they would do. I could barely contain my excitement.

I gathered Felix beside me on the sofa and sat down to read descriptions of what once had been. The entries were not in chronological order. They appeared to have been organized at some later date according to a criterion not readily discernible.

"Let's see. Where to begin?" I wondered. "Some of these are difficult to decipher." I selected an entry midway through the book written by a legible hand.

By fifteen aught three I was working in Italy and Leonardo DaVinci was painting the Mona Lisa. It took him years, if I recall correctly. His time with the young woman was limited by the watchful eye of her husband who, like I, suspected an interest between artist and subject more carnal than artistic. I would sit invisibly in my cloak to watch him paint.

He was remarkable. His brush expressed emotions DaVinci dare not give voice. His talent spoke those emotions in the expression of the young woman. The painting is a love story for all to see, paid for by a cuckold husband. It is not the artist's only sleight of hand. DaVinci is said to have embedded secret messages in many of his paintings. Codes of some forbidden knowledge perhaps, or jokes to amuse the cleverer of his patrons, or flights of fancy to satisfy his own imaginings in a world too rigid to contain him. Of this I know very little.

"Well, DaVinci never bothered to invent a decoder ring, so I'm iffy on the coding concept," I told Felix, and I swear he yawned. "Okay, enough with the random adulation. Let's find some action," I skimmed the next few paragraphs until I reached a more promising passage.

I had recently moved from plague-associated assignments in rural villages to city states like Tuscany. So many people smashed together in towns and markets gave me a fresh perspective on the human condition. They like to fight. Wars break out frequently and fisticuffs are everywhere. Even religion reforms itself into a source for murderous disputes. Vestiges of the Inquisition remain. And we have been given a name among the peasantry. I am seen henceforth as a grim reaper who visits too often amid the rich and poor alike.

Felix flicked his tongue impatiently.

"Okay, don't nag. I will get to a good part in a minute." I fluffed my pillows stalling for time while I paged for a story my pet might like.

A fortnight ago, I came to a village seated below a towering abbey. There lived a middle-aged friar with a fondness for sausage. The portly friar was never far from his heart's delight. He kept sausages in his pockets, hid them in his cell, and consumed them while performing his duties. Gluttony is a mortal sin, but alas, Friar Giovanni also harbored an abundance of pride, a craving to be elected Abbot of the abbey. His ambition was open for all to see as were his constant complaints regarding the resident Superior. Giovanni had decided a show of piety would give credence to his claim to the position. He made a show of foregoing sausage for the forty days of Lent. Given his unquenchable gluttony, his vowed abstinence was seen as a most pious act.

Not that Giovanni aspired to true piety. While gluttony may have been his favorite transgression, there was no sin the friar did not enjoy when an opportunity presented. The closest Giovanni ever came to virtue was a pretense of piety. One day it rose up and destroyed him as surely as the hand God might have done.

I was strolling through a vineyard when my wrist alerted me, my services were needed at the friar's abbey. I recall it was a holiday of some sort. Good Friday, I believe. Although I have never understood why the anniversary of a crucifixion was deemed 'good.' The nearest I have ventured to faith is a profound faith in the human capacity to be confusing.

"I'll give the man that," I interjected. A quick glance at Felix confirmed I had lost my audience. But I wanted to know how the story ended and continued to read aloud.

When I arrived, Friar Giovanni was on his bed, a sausage the size of his forearm protruding from his mouth. It was not a handsome sight. He was not yet dead, evidenced by the noises escaping from his impacted throat. According to the gossip shared among his brother friars, Giovanni had not been able to complete his Lenten vow. And when, on the final day of abstinence, his craving had bested him, the glutton had done so with abandon, shoving the sausage into his gullet with the urgency of a starving man.

The gossip seemed unlikely to me. Cloaked in invisibility I bent over the stricken friar and put a hand on his forehead to sense how he had arrived at such an uncomfortable situation. A moment later, I knew the truth. The Abbot had tired of Giovanni's ceaseless efforts to turn the friary against him and gone to confront Giovanni in his room. They had argued violently and when Giovanni took up a half-

eaten sausage and waved it weaponlike, the Abbot had shoved it down the friar's throat.

I watched his soul separate from the choking body and drift glumly to the corner of the tiny room. He had the look of a man betrayed by his dearest friend; the sausage not the Abbot. I guided the friar's essence to the assigned portal listening to him choke and gag the entire way although the murderous sausage had been left behind. To the best of my knowledge, sausage is not served in the afterworld, but I have the persistent impression Friar Giovanni was no longer interested even if it were.

The tome was my oxygen. I spent every available moment absorbed in its pages, learning every nuance I could about how other reapers behaved. I cherished their reactions, shared their amusement, and sought to match my behavior to theirs. I built a persona devoid of reaction to the messy occurrences reaping was witness to. My mind was a scythe cutting through the flotsam of human depravity. And I assumed myself no more than a weapon to cull the wicked.

As usual my assumption was incorrect. A fact made obvious by an entry that destroyed the wall I had built around my heart.

In the year 1851 anno domini, I attended the passing of a woman whose name, I believe will animate ages hence. She was a lady of words, an author of stories and an editor of the writing of others none the least of which was her husband.

She had been ill, suffered of a cancer that had fed upon her creative mind, leaving her thoughts to be found only in the books where she had confessed them. Those same books, which now bore witness and comfort to her final hours.

I was in London presiding over the transitions that stemmed from the birth of the industrial age when a name known instantaneously to me illuminated my wrist. It was the first day of February, and the weather was as harshly cold as the pain that pierced my heart upon seeing the identity of the soul I was to reap.

The room in which she lay was dimmed to the sparse light of a single candle. She saw me enter and gave me a faint smile which turned her face from ashen to a momentary glow of youth. I stood beside her bed, using my hood to hide me from all but her. But we were alone save for the few persons who entered from time to time—a physician and her son being those.

Touching her arm, I found no pain in the woman. Her senses were dulled by the disease, she yet knew death but waited her permission. And permission she gave, ready to partake of the mysteries she had pondered her full fifty-three years. Through my touch I learned that death had taken her mother at the woman's birth, her children save for the one son, and her husband in an accident from which the widow had never recovered.

It was the reaping of a friend I knew only from her books. A one-sided relationship as it were more intimate by its nature than any physical friendship could have provided. I alone between us mourned the imminent loss.

Her spirit rose above the bed and came to me unbidden.

"Will you take me to them?" she asked and I nodded.

Reapers are not privy to what lies beyond the portals. Thus, I can envision nought but joyous reunions for this woman who described the importance of the natural order of things in stories that bespoke a world of order and kindness.you Her greatest achievement warned humanity of the grave error of presuming the power of creation.

Clasping the hand that had written such truth, I led Mary Wollstonecraft Shelley to the portal and grieved this realm's loss as I watched her pass into the ages.

CHAPTER TWO

Friends in Low Places

"I am a performer of unpleasant tasks."

My lips edged into a slight smile as I said it. It is my customary response when asked. After all, it is an accurate, if nuanced, description of my profession. The young woman waitressing our table had finally given voice to the curiosity that had been banging about in her head for the past few weeks since Elly and I had been meeting for Saturday dinners at Tito's Bar.

Two things happened the moment after I said it. Elly choked on a sip of water and kicked my foot under the table. Darcy, our inquisitive waitress, looked to Elly, then at me and then fixed her gaze at the table. I watched as emotions skittered across her pretty young face while she attempted to decide if I was joking. People always do. No one ever chooses to merely accept the truth I offer. Which causes me to wonder why humans insist on asking questions at all.

"Unpleasant for whom?" Darcy bravely ventured a follow up.

"Not for us." Elly chuckled, managing an amused smile beneath a disapproving glance aimed at me. I shrugged and gave her foot a reciprocal nudge while politely asking Darcy to bring us the day's special.

"And two beers," Elly added when the girl walked away. "You are demented, Gwyn. You have been here what—all of six weeks. And you're already a cynic? Are you trying to convince people you are an assassin or a hooker?" She sat back and watched Darcy give us a final glance then slip into the kitchen. "I think she's leaning toward hooker."

"Informing people, I'm a reaper would elicit an even worse response." I pointed out. "Do you go around telling people you are a grim reaper?"

Elly's eyes widened. "Of course not. I tell them I am a nurse. Which I am most of the time. If you don't want to go there, why not just admit you work for the IRS?"

"Humans are not fond of taxes either."

Elly arched an eyebrow. "We all wondered why you chose the IRS for your day job, Gwyn. I mean really. You are a dainty little thing with curly hair and big puppy dog eyes. You look more like an ingenue than a tax collector!"

"Death or taxes," I chuckled. "The truth makes people feel doomed either way. Besides, I like the reaction I get. It stresses their complacency."

"I prefer them complacent," Elly shook her head. "Wait until you have a 300-pound lineman to gather up and wrestle to the portal. You will appreciate complacency."

I think Elly would have appreciated more complacency from me. Coaching a new reaper was not her favorite pastime. But she was dedicated in a militaristic sort of way. Not that she looked it. Elly was five foot nothing with soft curves, wavy blonde hair and a facetious smile that could disarm any challenge. Only the gravitas of her piercing blue eyes and my nearly inexhaustible need to know made me take her information seriously. That and the fact Elly had been a reaper since the Victorian Era. Elly had done it all. I on the other hand had barely done a thing. And I had questions; too many questions according to Elly. Having learned the who and what of my existence, I had turned my curiosity to a simple quest for *why*. Clearly, in Elly's mind, I was not a quick study.

Darcy returned with our dinner. She was in her early twenties, I guessed. Her light brown hair was bobbed at the collar and deep green eyes dominated a soft pixie face. She set down the plates and mugs and avoided looking at us.

"I am an accountant, Darcy." I told her in my most contrite voice.

She rewarded me with a genuine grin. "I knew it had to be something like that. The cook is my uncle. He refers to you as that pair of classy ladies. He likes that you come here once a week and takes particular care of your food. He said to tell you he hopes to meet you both one day."

"Thank you, Darcy." Elly offered using that devastating smile. "Please let him know I think the food here is delicious."

"Tell him to be careful what he hopes for," I suggested once Darcy walked off to assist other patrons.

Both Elly and I knew what Darcy did not. Her uncle was also a pimp who ran a lucrative drug distribution business in the back room. Uncle Pimp would be meeting one of us soon enough. I looked back to find Elly studying me.

"You feel sorry for the girl," she pointed out, then took a long, unsympathetic drink of beer. "I have learned the apple does not fall far from the family tree, Gwyn. You spend too much time processing lowlifes. It is time we upgrade your clientele. I can speak to Mr. Black for you."

Now there was topic that had worn out its welcome. Mr. Black, or Hades as I had learned while reading up on the beliefs of ancient humans, was Elly's not so secret ex-crush. She had the psychic bruises to prove it. And she was not alone. Mr. Black was notorious for his many dalliances with new reapers. I had a want-to/don't-want-to ambivalence about just meeting the guy. I had enough things to sort out without adding the vicissitudes of his or for that matter my own libido.

Elly and I lingered for an hour after dinner to discuss a cache of news she had been saving up. Mostly she wanted to discuss promotions; once again urging me to request an uplift to work with her. She did not so much want to work with me, I sensed. She wanted to groom me to replace her so that she could move on to an even more luxurious arrangement for herself.

I looked at the surrounds that had become comfortable to me. The place was definitely a dive situated on the west side of a city determined to disintegrate. But the manicured suburb Elly appreciated, that I assumed all reapers appreciated, seemed sterile in contrast. Elly thought me to be exactly like her, coolly ambitious. And in that moment, I assumed, I never would be.

The next morning, I awoke in a chair, the tome open in my lap and vague memories of having read a horrific story about a place named Pompeii. I climbed out of my chair and stretched then went to shower and dress. Felix had gone to his tank as I slept which meant I had either been mumbling or snoring loudly enough to displease him.

I turned on the shower and was about to shed my clothes when an intermittent buzzing sounded. Unable to place it at first, I checked my wrist plaz. Seeing no messages, I followed the sound to a drawer in an antique roll top desk in the corner of my bedroom. I retrieved a retro telephone and lifted the receiver awkwardly to my ear.

"Ah, hello?"

"Gwyn. There you are. I have been calling for days."

"Betz! What on earth are you doing contacting me on this, this outmoded device? Is your plaz not working?"

She responded with a chuckle. "No, I just wanted a more private conversation. They can access our communicators whenever they want, you know."

The hair on the back of my neck bristled at the hint of conspiracy in her voice. Betz was a reaper with a flair for cloak and dagger intrigue, usually unfounded. Nor had I a clue who this 'they' were. But I never venture into topics quite so fraught. I merely responded, "Uh-huh. So, what's up?"

"The conference, of course. I am freaking out. Two whole days away from the riff-raff. Had a collection at the butt crack of dawn this morning. Some little old man who transed in his sleep and didn't know whether to take his walker or order an Uber to head into the light. I never get the interesting trans you do. I escorted him to the portal, gave gramps a hug and sent him off."

"Fascinating," I lied, sinking into a chair and hooking one leg over the padded arm. Betz was the counterpoint to Elly. Having existed only a month or so longer than me, Betz was the nonconformist who kept my teeth on edge. She was tall and bold with dyed jet-black hair squared at her shoulders and tattoos adorning her biceps.

"One of my assignments wrung me out." It was best to match her story for story if possible. Above all, show no weakness.

"Eight victims, all scumbags. Some were decent enough to bleed out slowly, but still. It was grueling." I paused not really wanting to get into a prolonged gabfest. "Anyway. Please tell me the real reason you called on a peaceful Sunday morning."

The phone went silent for a moment. "Um, its actually afternoon, but okay, I will get to the point. Can I bunk with you?"

"No. Eh, I mean, let me think. Absolutely no. Why?" The last thing I needed was a roommate other than Felix.

"At the conference, silly!" Betz corrected me. "I am not dealing with that reptile of yours. Besides you are a slob."

I winced at the thought of the approaching coven. It was not an actual coven, of course. As far as I knew, witches were strictly an unproven human concept. Coven just seemed an appropriate description for a meeting of reapers. "When is it again?"

"You forgot didn't you! Next weekend. They are pairing us up in rooms, and I hope to choose you as my roommate. I don't really like most of the others—they're so morbid."

"Who'd have guessed."

"I know, right? You are the quiet type. Mostly off in your thoughts. It will be almost like being by myself."

"Thanks."

"My pleasure." Betz chuckled. "You know what I mean. Haven't you opened the packet they sent us? It explains the whole thing. Fifty of us are invited to a two-day discussion specifically for us new reapers. Do you really want to be roomed with some goodie two shoes?"

Betz was correct about that. There were tons of new reapers and most were as Betz implied, irritatingly obsessed with being accepted. It was highly likely the conference was meant to foster a sense of community between us. It was not something I especially wanted to do. But it occurred to me there might be an upside. The coven could be a chance to find the answers to my questions.

"Okay, sure. Let's do it. Thanks for suggesting it. And I promise not to bring Felix."

A few days later, I was hurrying along the sidewalk to a destination my wrist plaz directed me. It displayed an address near Darcy's pub and I prepared myself for a possibly ugly scene if the reaping involved the waitress' uncle.

The weather had cleared promising a pleasant evening and the streets were growing more active as the sun lowered. I hugged close to the building facades dodging the vagrants who were emerging from the shadows to begin their evening activities. I pulled the hood of my long cloak low over my face. It was the hood that provided me with invisibility, not the cloak as a whole; a fact I had learned in a most revealing manner.

I had also learned pale skin and unusual eyes rarely failed to garner attention in this part of the city. I had been propositioned more than once since my small apartment was situated just off skid row. Elly told me things were better in the suburbs, although what I witnessed of human nature made me doubt that. I saw no real difference between the population here versus the executive class who lived behind gated walls and manicured lawns.

I paused in an alley to lower my hood. The act of suddenly materializing, I discovered, tended to produce unpleasant reactions from bystanders and I did not want to frighten Darcy. Then I finger combed my hair and entered the dingy little eatery, making my way to my accustomed table at the rear where I checked my plaz. There was no new information about the person I was to collect. All I needed was a name; the rest would be obvious.

"How are you doing today, Miss Gwyn?" Darcy rushed over to set a frothy Guinness in front of me.

"Fine, thank you, Darcy." I replied then, unable to contain my curiosity, asked. "And you? Everything all right this evening?"

The waitress sighed. "You are a real lady, Miss Gwyn. No one seems to care about other people these days. Except for you. I am doing well, thank you. Could use a few more customers." She nodded to the handful of men scattered about the pub and sighed. "I could use a few more tips anyway. It has been slow. Even my uncle isn't here tonight."

I smiled, relieved her criminal uncle was evidently not the person I had been sent to collect. Darcy shown like a lamplight in the dismal squalor of downtown. I had hopes for her future and being tied down to run her uncle's pub if he died would be a tragedy.

"What are you, about twenty-two?" I asked. "You could do so much better than working here."

Darcy shrugged. "Just helping my uncle. He owns this place as you know. Mostly he just leaves it all for me to take care of unless he's cooking for you or a couple of his buddies. He says I talk about you all the time. This pretty lady who likes Guinness. He would still love to meet you."

I took a sip of beer to keep from chuckling. Bet he wouldn't. I wiped a spot of foam from my lip. "I won't be having anything to eat tonight, Darcy. Just stopped in for a quick drink. I have an appointment."

She nodded and wandered off to another customer and my attention turned to the others in the room. I amused myself seeing if I could spot my assignment before the name appeared on the plaz.

There were five men, most nursing beers and obviously thinking about various problems in their lives. A thin young man with a baby face sat by the front window nursing a glass of wine and watching people walking by. Probably dreaming about getting lucky. None of the men struck me as likely victims and none had an aura of malice. I spied an older man get up from the bar and head towards my table. He sat down opposite me and grinned an insincere grin.

"Penny for your thoughts, gorgeous," he said, reaching for my hand.

The touch brought with it a burst of information. The man harbored a deep desire for revenge. He wanted to harm someone, probably the person who had fired him. His thoughts were disorganized, bumping into each other with self-pity and anger vying for dominance in a boozy swirl. I gave a quick glance at my wrist. The name Paulo Menendez flashed with an updated time.

"That's a fancy watch you've got there, darlin'," he said, releasing my hand when the illumination ceased. "What the hell kind is it?"

"Go away." I felt irritated. The uninvited drunk was not the one I was assigned to collect.

"Now don't be like that. You are so gosh dang pretty, I must be seeing things." the man leaned forward. "My name is Joe. Can I buy you a drink?"

I scanned the others to confirm there was not a likely Paulo Menendez present. "I have one as you can see." The hairs on my neck pricked up and I knew my assignment would transition momentarily.

"Are you hungry then?" Joe continued. "Let me buy you a burger or something. You are such a skinny little thing."

I stood up and pushed my chair between us, a sense of urgency pulsing through me. My 'guest' seemed oblivious to my need to leave. He tugged on my cloak to get my attention. The act would have earned him a bloody nose if I had not been in such a hurry to get outside where I suddenly knew the transition would occur.

"You a vegan?" He continued. "I can get you a chicken sandwich if you like."

"No thanks."

I retrieved my cloak and Joe grabbed my arm attempting to hold me in place. "Hey, how about you give me a chance." His lips twitched as his brain sought a way to make the pretty woman stay. "At least tell me when I can see you again."

I turned and stared at his jaundiced eyes. I could almost hear his liver clogging. "Soon. I'd give it no more than a week or two," I told him, answering the question he hadn't exactly asked and definitely wouldn't have wanted to know. But ignorance is bliss as they say and Joe sank back into his chair with a pleased smile.

I dropped a twenty on the table for Darcy and another in sympathy for Joe then darted out of the pub just as the sound of a collision ripped through the air. It was dark out but I knew precisely where I needed to be without looking at the plaz. The intersection to my left was filling with a dense gray smoke illuminated by orange flashes as flames began to lick at the undercarriage of a crumpled vehicle. Sirens sounded in the distance and I joined the gathering crowd of onlookers.

I quickly saw there were two vehicles, a pickup and a sedan, that had blended into a single metallic mass. People were assisting the driver of the pick-up truck but the other driver claimed my attention. I could sense Paulo's erratic, heartbeat emanating from the crushed sedan. Within minutes a fire crew arrived and began using equipment trying to liberate Paulo from the center of the wreck. I followed the beat of Paolo's heart as it grew ever slower.

Suddenly there was a hand caressing my butt and the unmistakable scent of brimstone tickling my nose. There was only one being I'd been told of who would dare to do that—the so-called god of the underworld who controlled the realm beyond the portals.

"Get your hand off my ass, Hades."

"Tsk. Tsk. It is such a shapely ass, my dear. Must I?" Hades relocated his hand to my shoulder. "And I am Mr. Black these days. Hades is so millennia ago."

"Saw that movie, Hades. You are no Brad Pitt,"

He laughed. "These days one can be anyone they want. Strange times, my dear."

Mr. Black was correct. Fragmented identities and social engineering were creating a morass of untruths. Nothing magical or supernatural in human thinking. Only the sterility of technology and the pretense of fame and fortune. Curious, I turned to get a good look at the man. It was, Elly had said, exceedingly rare for Hades to attend a reaping.

"You doing pick-ups these days, Mr. Black?" I asked. "Or just out for a stroll?"

"I was hoping to find you, actually." He flashed a charming smile. "I heard about this ravishing new reaper who inexplicably got stationed in this," he waved a hand, ". . . this wretched location. There must have been a clerical error, my dear. Now that I see you, I can divine no other explanation. Slumming simply cannot be your style."

He was everything Elly had told me. He was dressed in a perfectly tailored pinstripe suit with a blue tie and singular goat's head pin on his lapel. His hair was combed back, and he was sporting a thin mustache. Mr. Black looked every inch the successful businessman—elegant, confident, and oozing a cynical charm.

I frowned. There were hundreds of questions I wanted to ask him, but I could sense Paolo was seconds from transition. I could not gather my attention away from my charge.

Black caressed my check gently. "So beautiful. And sexy as hell," he waggled his eyebrows. "And I know about hell."

I laughed out loud causing the people around us to glare in disapproval.

The sound of bending steel whined just then followed by the crash of metal as a large piece fell to the pavement. Black's demeanor changed abruptly. He snapped his fingers and the trunk of the sedan popped open. An officer lifted an unconscious child from the trunk and carry her to a gurney.

"I see they finally got the child out of the trunk." Hades said soberly. "No wonder you're feeling anxious, my dear." He snapped his fingers again and the sedan exploded, tossing the rescuers to the pavement, and roasting the vehicle's lone remaining occupant.

"A bit dramatic, don't you think?" I chided, noting Paolo's faint heartbeat had ceased at last.

Black laughed. "I love a cozy fire on a crisp night."

"It's June in California, Hades. It doesn't do crisp."

"It is whatever time or place we want it to be. You and I. We are not bound to the realities accepted by these unimaginative mortals." He noted a phantom drift up from the inferno in front of them. "Ah, Mr. Menendez has transitioned, I see."

"Did you want him to go? Or did you order delivery?"

Hades chuckled. "I have made arrangements." He nodded his head and the specter was led away by two of his minions. "There. Now we have the evening to spend in more pleasant pursuits."

"I have a headache." I lied and tapped my wrist verifying the event had completed.

"You are a headache, my dear. But you will never experience one." Black clarified. "What you do have is the pleasure of taking dinner with me tonight. I shall endeavor to ply you with wine until you fathom the possibilities of us."

"They warned me about you, Mr. Black."

"You would do better to be warned about wagging tongues, my dear."

He put his arm about my waist and steered us away from the gaggle of on-lookers who also started to drift away from the carnage.

"I know you have questions, Gwyn. And who better than I to answer them?"

I sighed. He was mesmerizing and I almost went with it. Then the look on Elly's face when she had told me about him came to mind and I shook my head. "I, ah, I hope to get my answers at the conference this weekend. You know, it is not a great idea to mix work and, ah, pleasure."

He flashed an endearing smile. "I prefer all play and no work. And I spared you some work tonight. I could have cooked them both. The pedophile and the child. Imagine the paperwork." He studied me for a long moment. "I think I'm going to enjoy a game of hard to get with you, Gwyn."

Then he was gone.

My executive assistant would have made a terrific offensive lineman if she had been a decade younger, a foot taller . . . and a man. Liz was as stout as she was short, five-by-five of solid attitude, but her heart was pure gold. The woman managed my calendar, kept the files neat as a library, and offered an endless stream of unsolicited but undeniably pertinent advice. She even consoled weeping clients as they left my office with a payment plan for back taxes and ever so occasionally Liz told me to whom I should give a break.

It was her efficiency that made me acquiesce to her request for a small television at her work station. Liz loves her news, particularly news of disasters of which there was ample supply. I suspect she awoke every morning wondering what had blown up. She was rarely disappointed. The TV seemed always to be filled with footage of some unfortunate situation.

I arrived at my office to find Liz engrossed in a flood occurring halfway around the planet. She was munching on a large bag of Takis; eyes glued to the screen, earpiece stuck in her ear feeding her adrenalin high.

She deposited a pair of tax evaders into the chairs fronting my desk and set a packet of information in front of me—tapped it three times with her finger, letting me know her judgment concerning the couple. It was a code between us. One tap meant give them a break. Two taps meant make them pay. The rarely used triple tap meant give them hell. If she only knew!

Having reviewed the case several times, I shared my assistant's point of view. Mr. and Mrs. Lynche operated a highly profitable LLC which produced low quality goods manufactured in third world sites. They washed the profits through a network of pseudo entities. Liz had unraveled the Lynche's holdings with her customary bull-doggedness. I let the couple sit in silence while I thumbed through the report Liz had prepared. Closing the folder, I had to chuckle. Liz would have made a superlative reaper. It was clear she was delivering the Lynches to hell.

"I assume you've spoken with our attorney," Mr. Lynche said, elevating the last word as if the comment were a question.

It happens that I despise that affectation. He got a simple response "Yep."

"The audit must have been performed by some overreaching clerk," his wife pointed out. "There is no possible way we owe any money."

Stone faced, I remained silent, seeing no point in debating the issue. I was working on very little sleep and had my own issues to deal with. When Mr. Lynche read whatever he read in my eyes, he cleared his throat and attempted a verbal backflip.

"Of course, my wife wasn't referring to you in specific." He chanced a quick smile.

I slid a piece of paper across the desk to him. It was a bill for $432,679.15. It was not well received.

It may have been my imagination but the man seemed to pale while the woman turned quite red. Suggesting to me once again that opposites do attract. Beneath the torrent of expletives bursting from the Lynches, I could hear the low rumble of Liz's singular chuckle.

It was taco Tuesday night at the card room and I was in the mood to celebrate the demise of the Lynches by having a bit of fun. I stopped by my apartment to shed my business suit and don a pair of jeans and a tight T-shirt. Although I was rather good at poker, I had no qualm about using any diversion available. Something about a pair of breasts derails the ability of human males to think logically. The skies were clear revealing a canopy of stars only partially obscured by the city lights. I parked at the rear of the lot, set the car alarm I had had installed in my aging Chevy, and jogged to the rear door of the dingy little card room.

The tables were nearly full so I skipped the tacos and ordered a diet Coke going straight to the cashier to buy some tournament chips. Two of the players recognized me and we exchanged waves as we waited for the dealer to shuffle.

Poker is a study in patience, math, and luck. The first two are easy enough; luck is the variable that causes all the trouble. Humans seem to worship luck as a deity, believing luck answers their prayers or protects them in some undefinable way. It is not linked to behavior. It does not weigh the character of those who seek it. Luck just happens. And every time I play poker, I assume luck will happen to me.

The first round contained nothing of particular interest. There were no bad beats and no note-worthy bluffs. There were merely twenty-seven hands terminating with pairs and one flush in clubs. The banter was friendly enough consisting of light-hearted exchanges of silly jokes and comments on the weather. Poker players do not discuss serious topics. They study each other looking for tells or patterns that can help them avoid being bluffed.

I had the other eight players read within the first ten minutes. It occurred to me during the break that I should test my opponents with higher bets. But then I remembered I just wanted to relax and have a little fun. My stomach growled and I returned to the table wishing I had not skipped the tacos.

We lost two players in the second round; young bucks who went all in and ended up all out. One of the better players by my estimation nearly went out on a bad beat. I felt sympathy for the guy. Bad beats are my singular weakness in poker. I get reckless for a few hands as if the poker gods were expected to apologize for the damn ace on the river that bested my kings. A metaphysical explanation is easier to deal with than accepting one's error in judgment. At least it is for me.

As we were about to go to final table, I was sorely tempted to go all in with trips after the flop. But I didn't. We were on the bubble and among my remaining opponents was the guy who had suffered the bad beat. Suspecting the poker gods might decide to apologize to him, I folded when he challenged my raise, preferring to take us both to final table where he would at least make some money for the evening.

"Thanks," he said walking up to me during the next break.

"You're welcome, Jason." I surprised him earning a curious look. "You look like a Jason." I smilingly explained. Actually, I had heard someone call him that name earlier.

"Is that a good thing?" he asked. "If we follow your rules, I will have to call you beautiful. And that was a pretty beautiful thing you did for me in there. You had me beat, didn't you?"

"Turns out I did. But I wasn't positive at the time."

We shook hands.

"May I buy you a drink? After the final round, I mean." He asked.

He was so sincere I nearly accepted. Jason was a pleasant enough looking guy. Before I could answer, the bell rang calling us back to our table. While we played, I considered accepting his offer. Unfortunately, we had touched hands and I knew precisely where spending time with Jason would end. He had been married twice already and had two kids to support. He was compulsive and unlucky. I folded on Jason without regret.

Jason came in third in the tournament. I was second. I did not repeat my generosity and I am certain he did not expect me to. The winner had been visited by luck which accounted for his placement. As soon as we got our payouts, I slipped out the back and got into my car. I saw Jason pause on the patio and look around then shake his head and return to the tables to lose his winnings.

It was after eleven when I stopped at the all-night liquor store a few blocks from my apartment. With any luck, I reasoned the night clerk might have remnants of a pot of decaf still hot and I could grab a donut or a sandwich to make up for the skipped tacos. I felt empty inside. Anything would do so long as I did not look at the sell-by date.

"Huh?" I rubbed my eyes then refreshed the screen. The same coordinate reappeared and I realized I was standing right where the plaz wanted me. Convinced it had to be an error, I did a quick visual check around me. There were no bodies or impatient specters. The only being in the place was the clerk sitting on a stool behind the counter, paging through a magazine. He was an older man whom I had seen numerous times. Not particularly friendly but efficient and willing to work nights in this part of the city. His name came to me- Craig! I recalled him saying something once about helping his grandson buy a car. I watched him for a moment; he looked fine and ignoring the plaz, I went on about my business.

I was deciding between ham and cheese or tuna salad when the bell above the entry door dinged and two men rushed in. They went directly to the counter and demanded money. Craig stood up and time slowed down. I saw the men lower their hands, reaching for the guns hiding in their pockets. Simultaneously, Craig raised his hand, a gun already in it. He fired twice and both of his customers dropped to the floor. My chin dropped at the same moment.

Craig sat back down and resumed reading his magazine just as time resumed its normal pace. Two specters rose up and drifted to the door. I went to collect them, passing briefly by the counter to check on the clerk. Craig stood and asked me if I needed anything.

"Ah, no, no, thank you." I said moving toward the door. "I just came in to pick up a few things." My gaze shifted to the lifeless bodies bleeding beneath a rack of assorted bags of chips.

"Sorry about the mess," Craig told me. "I'll call someone to clean that up after I finish my article." He sat back down and resumed his reading.

I motioned for the spirits of the two inept thieves to follow me.

"Now why would we want to do that, lady?" One of the men snorted.

"Because you're dead."

Never Ask a Question You Don't Really Want the Answer To

dug through a stack of mail looking for the packet Betz had mentioned. The conference was tomorrow; I had run out of procrastination time. Procrastination? Hell, I had put the coven entirely out of mind. My administrative assistant ended the work week at 5:55 p.m. by telling me she had cleared my calendar for Monday next in case my "weekend vacation" proved to be exhausting. Then she laughed and instructed me to have a good time. Vacation my ass, I almost blurted out. But I merely thanked her and made a beeline for my apartment.

The packet had slid behind the desk. I got on my knees, reached out and grabbed it and moaned when I felt the heft of the envelope. I consoled myself with the idea there might be useful information in it I needed. Like the location of the conference. Betz had taken care of the room reservation but I had not bothered to ask where it was being held. My plaz would not help me unless someone decided to transition right in front of the appointed hotel tomorrow morning. Which was unlikely.

I sat at the desk and sorted through the packet contents. I pulled out a badge. A Badge! Really? Like reapers were not capable of learning names with a touch or suffered from some memory flaw, well, it was best not to dwell on that point. Not to mention reapers looked like reapers. At least to other reapers.

Meal menus were in the packet with information on how to submit your order prior to the convention. I tossed the menus and resolved to bring some snacks. Although starvation seemed less likely a fate than boredom when I skimmed the list of topics for each of the sessions. That dire assumption quickly dissipated when I opened the last item, it was a pamphlet; four pages of what could be titled *Reaping for Dummies.*

The first page listed specific tools made for reapers. I felt my eyebrows elevate as I read the list and jotted down notes for several.

A reaper's role is a delicate balance of duty, compassion, and efficiency. Equipped with the following tools and skills, a resilient reaper guides souls to the afterlife ensuring that the journey from life to death is managed with the utmost professionalism.

Page One:

TOOLS

Plaz: *Device embedded beneath the skin of the left wrist. It records the identity of souls collected and serves to alert reapers of an assignment including name, time, and location. It also can be used as a communication device.*

Cloak: *Provides anonymity and mystery. When worn with the hood up, it renders a reaper invisible to humans.*

Hourglass: *Symbolizes the measure of time remaining in a human's life.*

Scythe: *The scythe symbolizes the severing of soul from body. Mainly symbolic in the current era, the scythe presents as a cane when carried.*
Talisman: *A protective charm used to ward off malevolent forces or navigate different realms.*
Portal Key: *Technological device to open portals between realms. Currently on back order.*
Lantern: *Represents light in the darkness. Can be used to guide recalcitrant souls to a portal.*

I looked around to see if the devices were in my apartment. A dusty hourglass sat atop a kitchen cabinet, and there was an innocent-looking cane in my bedroom closet. The talisman and portal key were still at large when I returned to continue with the pamphlet.

Page Two:

SKILLS

Empathy: *Understanding the emotional states of the newly deceased.*

I skimmed through the rest: Discretion, Time Management, Emotional Stability. Yatta. Yatta. I was created a reaper. I either had those qualities or I did not. Reading about them seemed an unlikely way to attain them.

The third page was filled with drawings of cloaked reapers leading souls through the dark to a portal, and motivational cliches. Of special interest were the recommended reassurances a reaper could use to calm the newly dead.

"Think of the afterlife not as a final destination, but as an intricate process of recycling your essence."

Not much comfort to a soul expecting to meet up with dearly departed Aunt Mae.

"Consciousness like all energy cannot be destroyed, only transformed."

"Seen through the lens of science, consciousness is a fundamental aspect of the universe, akin to space, time, and matter."

Those words did not fit in my mouth. I am more likely to say "Enjoy hell, you slimy bastard." Or "I hope everything works out for you." Actually, I rarely said anything to the spirits.

The pamphlet had not answered the question I struggled with most. Why? Why were reapers necessary? Humans should be able to navigate themselves to a portal, the old 'go into the light' idea. I could spend my time drinking Mai Tais on a beach while humans came and went as they pleased. After all this time why hadn't humans figured out the cycle of karma and reincarnation. They should pull up their soul socks and head into the recycler all by their lonesome.

Setting aside the plight of humanity, I realized my real questions had to do with my own species. Reapers. Are we immortal? What happens if we just chuck the whole thing and stop performing what seemed a repetitive agenda? I once read that a bullet shot in space continues on forever because the universe is expanding faster than a bullet is propelled. Maybe my questions are like bullets. They will never reach an answer. They proceed into the universe unrequited toward an unachievable destiny.

The last page of the pamphlet offered no answers but did set a tone. I think it was meant to be merely informative, but there was an undeniable threatening aspect. Reapers must:

Never reveal your true identity.
Never intervene on behalf of a human.
Never fail to complete an assignment.

Or else what? I wondered. The information in the pamphlet was like the stuff I had read on the PC; long on statements, short on explanations. But I did discover the answer to one of my questions, the conference was at the Marriott in Burbank. As to the rest, not so much.

I returned the items to the envelope giving the program a final look. The coven would commence with a meet and greet at nine o'clock Friday night. My head exploded. I should have checked. I had just assumed it would begin Saturday morning. Jumping to my feet, I checked the time. It was 6:30 p.m. There was plenty of time to get there if . . . I saw Felix staring up at me. Shit! I have one trustworthy companion and I could not abandon him without his bedtime story.

I took a quick shower and threw some clothes into a duffle bag. Felix sashayed into the bedroom and settled on the nightstand. He was devoted to being on time, expecting nothing less from me, and it was clear he wanted his story. He was the perfect critic; silent in both approval and disappointment. I grabbed the tome and sat cross-legged on the bed.

"I found a story I think you will like, Felix. It has the action you enjoy and one of your ancestors plays a role." And it's relatively short.

Felix shrugged into a lazy coil and rested his head to stare at me in happy anticipation. I opened the ancient reaper's tome and turned to a page in the middle.

"The Spanish invasion of the Incas began about 1525 anno domini. It promised to become deadly and I was transferred to the Andes just as it began. The first assault was the introduction of smallpox inadvertently brought by the Spanish conquistadors.

A large portion of the Inca population perished from the disease including Emperor Huayna Capac. His sons fought a civil war over control which eventually went to Atahualpa.

"The military defeat of the empire took decades, but once Pizarro arrived things went downhill quickly. I worked around Cusco harvesting the souls of Inca and Spanish alike. But soldiers do not die only in battle. Some are victims of their own misadventures. Juan Oliverio Bigotes was such a conquistador."

Felix yawned.

"Hey, the guy's name is important, Felix. First because Bigotes means whiskers and the man was rat like enough to have had actual whiskers. Second, his initials were JOB. You know, like the hard-luck guy in the Bible. I assure you; this JOB was no biblical good guy. On the contrary Bigotes was a master at accumulating wealth by taking it from others. He stole sheets of gold from the walls of temples and jewelry off the bodies of the fallen warriors. Not to mention from the homes of women and children. He would have been a wealthy man if he had gotten home to Spain."

"The deceitful conquistador hid his ill-gotten spoils in leather bags made from the hide of local animals. He was partial to snake skin because of its smooth feel and ability to shed water."

Felix hissed, lifting his head obviously disturbed by such a violation of decency.

"Abandoning his position in the battlefield, JOB slithered back to the Sacsayhuaman fortress where

I was watching the engagement and waited for what I was sure would be the onset of a multitude of assignments. Battles meant busy days for reapers. I was draped in my cloak, thus invisible to humans when Senor Bigotes slinked past me carrying an armful of gold chains pilfered from the fallen warriors.

"No sooner had he stepped past me then my wrist lit up with his name. I followed him as he climbed higher and crouched down to remove small rocks from the base of the high, zigzag wall.

"He dug furiously, pulling bag after bag from a sizeable hole he had created in the stone wall. If the Inca had fathomed the depth of their invader's greed, they would have reinforced their imposing edifice. As it was, walls that could survive earthquakes yielded all too readily to human intention."

I paused to see if Felix was still sulking about my earlier revelation. He had relaxed down into a lazy coil looking no worse for the shock.

"Bigotes untied the thin rope used to enclose a tube-shaped bag with a distinctive pattern and began stuffing his latest acquisitions into it. The air was pierced with a high-pitched shriek as the thief jumped to his feet. Hanging from his hand was a large Fer-de-Lance whose skin matched that from which the bag had been fashioned."

Felix reared up and swayed rhythmically from side to side. It was a tour-de-force of reptilian applause. I clapped my hands in return. "I knew you would like this story, Felix. Do you think it was the scent or the bag that had attracted the snake? I like to think it was an act of revenge, brilliantly executed, for a brother who had been slaughtered for the conquistador's wicked purpose. But that's just me."

Taking refuge in his cage, Felix was silent on the matter.

How many reapers can fit in a resort is a question no one ever asked. There were pale-eyed attendees everywhere when I arrived at the hotel. I refused to count them but there were many more than the fifty newbies Betz had told me to expect. Nor did I look at the maximum occupancy plaques. I already knew I was amidst many more reapers than I cared to be.

I checked in and went directly to my room finding evidence Betz had already arrived. There was a note on what I assumed was my designated bed, telling me to join them in the Galaxy Ballroom ASAP. Them? I had arrived late but it still was surprising to see my roommate had assembled an entourage. I checked my duffle bag for something to wear to what seemed to be a more formal event than the agenda had implied. I slipped into a simple black cocktail dress, added a gold chain at my waist and heels and spent a few minutes freshening my makeup.

The foyer was crowded with reapers gathered in little groups renewing acquaintances and speculating on what the conference would provide. I spied a trio heading to the reception and followed them down a long corridor then, on a hunch, I made an abrupt left into a bar just outside the ballroom.

"I told you!" I heard Betz gloat as I approached. She was at the bar accompanied by a pair of reapers, the names of which came up blank to me.

"Told them what?" I asked squeezing into place beside her.

"That you'd eventually show up," she said handing me a glass of Guinness. "I knew you'd be late and prefer a bar to the reception. "Did you find my note?"

I nodded and sipped my drink while they chitchatted. I paid enough attention to pick up the names of the two reapers she was with. After half an hour, I had learned the reception was open to all interested reapers in the Southwest district. I wondered if Elly was among the growing throng. Betz was having a grand time being plied with more free drinks than she could possibly consume. I was on my second Guiness, which I purchased myself, and suffering the noise volume assailing my ears. As people continued to squeeze into the room, I had the distinct impression the walls were closing in around us.

This all came to a sudden halt when an elegant woman walked in and clapped her hands. Instant silence. If the woman was reaper, she was not a newbie. She looked to be in her fifties, severe, and reeking of authority. I had no idea who she was, but evidently the others knew her. She uttered not a word but, as if commanded, the bar began to empty. I followed the reapers to an immense room set up for dining. I glanced at Betz who shrugged, all trace of her hopes for a fun-filled weekend having faded from her face.

We found ourselves at different tables once we located our individual seating cards which not only had our names but the sentence 'Attendance at all lectures and work sessions is mandatory.' It was printed in goldleaf. No one can ignore goldleaf. The crowd had thinned to fifty newbies and a score of old timers whose accomplishments were sufficiently dazzling to be shared with the new kids.

I was seated at a table with four reapers I had never met. Two were males, new like me; the others were females who had been reaping for centuries. They were probably part of the World War II expansion, I assumed incorrectly as usual. I wondered if reapers were created en masse rather than one at a time, and added the idea to my mental list of questions I dared hope would be answered by the end of the conference.

To my relief, I was served the full meal despite my dereliction in submitting my menu choices. The first course, a lovely blackberry chicken salad, was attended with the exchange of pleasantries; mainly comments regarding the weather, sports scores, and vacation venues. When the main course arrived, the eldest of my companions put the verbal fluff aside and announced she had been a reaper during the time of the Roman conquests. What, I wondered, did she find most rewarding about being a reaper?

Her name was Demea. She glanced at me and smiled. I would have sworn she recognized me for an instant, then turned away. It was a snub although I had no idea why.

"What I enjoy most are the truly gruesome assignments." Demea announced. "There were days when we literally waded in blood gathering the dead from battlefields. It was glorious."

I blinked at the rare prime rib on my plate and stifled a gag, resisting the urge to see if she was still wearing her cherished gore-laden boots.

Saturday, the appointed day of lectures, began at the end of a dreamless sleep. I rubbed my eyes only to find I was alone. Betz must have been otherwise entertained for the night, or there was a passed-out goth body somewhere because, bolder than I, Betz had probably found a way to ignore the goldleaf mandate.

The door swung open and my bedraggled roommate stumbled in. She tossed a bag on her empty bed before flinging herself after it.

"Don't tell me you wanted to be late again, Gwyn," she accused snorting as she laughed.

"Tell me you're not drunk again," I retorted, pushing back the covers, and heading to the shower.

"I may be slightly drunk, but you're going to be late. We have ten minutes to get downstairs to the meeting room. I don't think you'll make it. I . . ."

The rest went unheard as I stuck my head under the water, did a quick soap and rinse and turned the water off. Betz was still talking.

"I wonder if they punish reapers somehow?" she mused. "I mean what can they do to us?"

"My mother told me 'Never ask a question you don't really want the answer to'," I told her.

Betz sat up and rubbed her temples. "You didn't have a mother, Gwyn."

"Maybe that's why I ask so many questions."

I grabbed a fresh blouse and slacks from my duffle and dressed commando style when I saw I had neglected to pack underwear. I arranged my hair and applied a minimum of makeup before slipping a room key and the day's agenda into my pocket and heading for the door. Betz was at my heels, buttoning a fresh blouse as we jogged tothe elevator.

We blended with another group of stragglers and took seats at the front of the lectern. Betz dropped her head into hands with a moan.

"You're still drunk, I see."

"True that," Betz whispered. "And you're . . ."

"Not late." I grinned.

Mr. Black walked to podium and the room drifted quiet. He was dressed in a blue shirt and black trousers. No tie. None of the aristocratic costuming he wore when we had met. Yet he was ridiculously handsome and charm bled off him in nearly visible waves.

"Good morning, reapers. If you tap your plaz five times, you will regain sobriety quickly. It is a feature I added decades ago, the better to command your undivided attention."

Hushed clicks echoed in the room and Betz sighed with personal relief. Mr. Black looked at me and winked.

"Better?" The handsome speaker smiled at the suddenly attentive faces peering up at him. "By the way, you can use the five tap method to correct any other discomfort you may experience.

"Most of you have been here only a month or so. So, there is quite a lot of information you have not had the experience to discover. Facts are a poor substitute for experience. But it is hoped knowing the facts will be enough to guide your activities. To get things started, I am going to talk about three things: humans, the system, and the future.

"Humans are an important species. They have their foibles but they are young as the cosmos goes and they are progressing. Each human life contributes to creation. Each death completes a cycle and after some readjustment begins a new existence. Life and death are not opposites, they are parts of a continuous flow. You maintain that flow. My realm manages the raw, so to speak, materials."

Hands flew up and Mr. Black motioned them down. "I won't be taking questions," he said, his eyes having tracked to mine. He winked then went back to his presentation.

"Yes, reapers have superior skills and knowledge, but not merely for your personal enjoyment. Reapers have completed the kind of evolution in which humans are now engaged. Reapers exist because of humans, not the other way around. Sorry about the ego deflation, people. But it is what is it. Which brings me to my second topic. The system.

Creation is an orderly, continuous process. Having created itself, the universe demands to repeat the process creating life forms and adjusting its own awareness in an endless system of renewal. The raw materials spring from energy which is the source of creation. In our corner of existence, humans learn, reapers manage their transition to me, and my minions release human consciousness back into the cosmos to reassemble into whatever species or form is required."

Mr. Black paused to take a sip of water and I used the moment to interject.

"So, you manage a recycling center and we are, well, essentially trash collectors."

My comment was met with a low, rumbling gasp and a pair of dark eyes pinning me to my chair with their intense disappointment. *Et tu, Gwyn?* I had wounded him somehow through a connection I did not understand.

"That's a theory worthy of an adolescent human philosopher," Mr. Black chastised me. "Consciousness is hardly trash. Would you rather yours was returned in fragments to the void of space?"

That stung more than a little somewhere deep in my brain. I may not remember a past, but I had plans for a future and silence seemed the better course. Mr. Black took another sip of water and let me stew in my embarrassment for a long, uncomfortable moment before moving on to the last of his three topics.

"The system is undergoing a change. That is primarily why you are here. Not here at a meeting, but here on this planet at this moment. In the last 14,000 years, humans have experience twenty catastrophes seriously imperiling their progress. Five of those disasters have occurred since 2004, That's twenty-five percent in a handful of years. Clearly the pace is quickening. Combined with the exponential growth in population, it does not take a genius to see the situation is dire indeed.

"Aside from increasing the number of reapers, we are updating the complex process and the portals between our realms. You will be given new capabilities in the next few days. You are going to need them. Learn them well and apply yourself to improving your contribution to the system."

Mr. Black paused; his face steeled in concern. He was reading the room and did not fancy the plot. We were not ready in his estimation. I could have told him we were green. We were little more than children, performing tasks according to an instinct that was given not earned.

"He closed his eyes momentarily, then opened them and looked directly at me again. "Many of you question the purpose of your existence. Why are there reapers? Why do humans even die? The best answer I can give you is, you are part of a system that has worked successfully for eons. Ready or not, it is up to you to ensure its future."

Exhausted after sitting through six hours of droning lectures and making nice during the breaks with reapers who wanted to continue the discussion, I ditched Betz and fled to our room. If she got lucky, she would not be back for hours. If I got lucky, I would again have the room all to myself for the entire night. Turned out we were both fortune's child. I awoke to a hot Sunday morning and an empty hotel room.

I showered and chose a pair of jeans and a silky blouse for the day. The agenda, stated cloaks were mandatory, a requirement I found completely absurd. It was in the eighties by 9:30 a.m. and would only be growing hotter as the day went on. I had learned the hard way wearing only my cloak was considered a faux pas but the thought of fifty naked reapers in the room amused me. I clipped the fastener at my throat and swooped the sides of the cloak behind my shoulders grateful for the air-conditioned auditorium where the first of our work sessions was scheduled.

Viewing a sea of black cloaks as I entered the room, I recalled why I had dubbed these meetings covens. This event had all the earmarks of witchcraft except for the sacrifice and brooms. Just to be sure, I gazed around the room. Finding not a broom in sight, I took a seat in the back row.

A video walked us through new features evidently loaded or activated in the plaz overnight. Betz had been correct. They, whoever they were, could and did listen in to us via the communication device. Now we could reach them as well. We could ask questions on the plaz and they would respond. I had plenty of questions. But I could not recall a single assignment during which I would have needed to ask a question about the reaping. Still, it was a novel idea.

"Told you, they were listening," Betz plunked herself into the seat beside me and whispered.

"Indeed, you did," I acknowledged noting the elegant epaulets on her shoulders and the satin piping she had added to the plain black cloak. "What is this? Are we supposed to personalize these things?"

"No, no. I need a fancy costume for a Halloween party," she blushed. "I love parties. Can't show up as a reaper, you know. So, I hauled out my cloak and glammed it."

"You want to go as a doorman?" I laughed.

"A vampire." She explained shimmying her shoulders. "Vampires are not real, Gwyn. So, I used my imagination."

"Neither are reapers if you ask a human." I replied. "Grim Vampire is sort of a double negative."

"Which makes a positive," she retorted. "Besides, I like the way it looks. Kind of official, you know. Makes the transitioners want to follow me."

I simply sighed. Somewhere in her twelve weeks on Earth, Betz had lost the whole concept of grim reaper-ness and become a tour guide.

The lights dimmed and a video came up on the giant screen, starting with a map of the SoCal district. The map showed the locations of portals scattered across the geography. I had no idea there were so many. The portals were color-coded like stop lights. The color indicated the portal's availability status: green meant a portal was open, yellow indicated the portal was reserved, and red meant a portal was not yet open. What struck me immediately was the fact nearly a third of the portals were red.

At first blush, the dramatic increase in the number of portals could indicate humanity was in for a rough time, maybe extinction. They were subject to that if history is any indication. Plagues, wars, natural disasters were continually taking their toll. My reaction was to think the IRS needed to shorten its payment plans. If people were going to be dropping like flies, the government should grab the money as quickly as possible. My second thought about the IRS was I really did not give a damn. I was going to be too busy reaping mounds of newly dead to ruined some living person's day. Working for the IRS was a cover not a career.

The better question was, is this a regional thing? Or was the whole planet about to get hit? I wanted to know and turned up my plaz to ask when Betz stopped me. She shook her head and put a finger to her lips.

"Never ask a question," she whispered without needing to explain why she believed that.

Three work sessions filled the remainder of the day. I tuned in and out. The group reapings where dozens of us coordinated at a catastrophe put my lack of multitasking ability on display. I eavesdropped on Betz while she flirted with a reaper named Troy telepathically until it got raunchy. I jammed my plaz twice while practicing the new features and momentarily consi-dered cutting off my arm. But it would probably grow back, so I didn't.

By the time the day ended, all I wanted was a hot bath and quiet chat with Felix. Neither of which were in the cards. Betz threw a gothic tantrum when I hinted at skipping the after party. Which was unfortunate, since the party fairly rocked and I did not. Evidently a catastrophe was not a topic of great concern to the others. Watching them frolic on the patio using their hoods to startle innocent passersby, I found myself wondering about the future. An hour in, Betz discovered me in a corner peacefully nursing a port and danced over to rescue me.

"Gwynie, darlin', come join us." Betz pleaded. Her friends from the bar, Paul and Drake, were with her. Drake took my hand and started to gyrate to the music.

"I'm not in the mood," I said as politely as I could, eager to conceal what were undoubtedly my two left feet. My head was swimming with questions I wished would go away and my mood was dissipating rapidly. Drake guided me to the bar, bought me a drink and left me to my musings.

Betz leaned to whisper in my ear. "You look positively grim!"

"We are supposed to be grim." I snapped back. "I'm going to get you business cards to remind you."

"Oh, tsk, tsk." she straightened up. "So, something's up. Who cares??"

"Then what happens to us afterward?" I asked. It was infuriating no one seemed to put it together. Fewer humans had to mean fewer reapers. "We got changes today.The whole system is changing and I still haven't fathomed the current system. No one is bothering to ask us what we think. They have not even told us specifically what is coming. An earthquake, a meteor, some particularly revolting plague?"

Betz started to laugh. "Christ, Gwyn, you have a gift for the dramatic. Put a cork in it would you? It's our last night to party. You have something against having fun?"

Drake laughed. "Don't let Mr. Black's words get to you, Gwyn. What the devil does he know?"

"Everything!" Mr. Black's deep voice interjected. "At least much more than you could possibly conceive of, dear boy."

"Speak of the devil," Betz commented under her breath. "Where the hell did he come from?"

Mr. Black grinned. "Precisely, Betzy. For the record, I am not the devil. For one thing I am much better looking. Secondly, Lucifer is one of hell's lieutenants, I am the CEO of the underworld."

He was dressed all in black with his collar open and his tie stylishly loose. The look suited him. Devil or not, Mr. Black was extremely sexy. He moved over to the bar and stood by my side. I could hear his heart beating and feel the air move with the long, deep breaths he was taking.

"You look lovely tonight," he purred, displaying no evidence of a residual disappointment at my unfortunate remark during his speech.

He snapped his fingers and I found myself in the center of a magnificent room in what could have been a medieval castle by the North Sea. The room was huge with a high arched ceiling and stone floor covered in places by thick rugs in shades of blue and green. The furniture was gathered into sitting areas, one set beside a massive fireplace with an ornately rendered mantel. The room was breathtaking in its opulence yet warm and inviting. The air was scented with spices and I felt my senses begin to swoon. The room was an architectural representation of Mr. Black himself.

Candlelight revealed my host standing across the room, pouring wine into a pair of tall crystal glasses.

"Planning on seducing me?" I asked.

He chuckled and handed me one of the glasses. The contents were delicious.

Appreciating the look of bliss on my face, Mr. Black told me, "You never could resist Malbec Cuvee, especially 1947."

I looked at him puzzled.

He gave me an enigmatic grin. "I have an excellent memory."

"Of a night that never happened? You definitely have quite a vivid imagination!"

He smiled. "Of a night that almost did. I like to involve myself in things you cannot resist." He refilled my glass.

In a contest between a pitchfork and a scythe, put your money on the scythe. It has a longer snath and a vicious blade. Mr. Black was the pitchfork, capable of little pricks and stabs of knowledge. I thought myself the scythe ready to sweep his attentions aside.

"I can assuredly resist you!"

Black had a fondness for crystal. Specimens of every type and color sparkled in the soft light creating an incredible warm glow. It was almost angelic. Tapestries covered the walls, each perfect in its complexity and design. They dated from various epochs—ancient oriental works to the ages of Europe. There were artifacts from primitive South and North American tribes.

"What did you mean a night that almost happened?" I asked, suddenly, feeling inexplicably familiar with the artifacts.

He sat in a huge padded chair and followed me with his eyes. He seemed to enjoy my reactions and took note of the items which interested me most. He lowered the background music and provided a dialog describing the source and purpose of each item that caught my interest.

"I've wanted you to visit this place for so long," he said when I finished my tour.

"I did not expect hell to be quite so beautiful," I admitted. Of course, I had never crossed a portal and entered this realm, but humans do not speak well of the place. "If you're trying to impress me, it's working."

"I was hoping you would like it." He motioned to a chair opposite his.

I sat down and set my wineglass on the little table beside the chair. The opulence of the room, the wine, even the sound of Black's voice was having an effect on me. I closed my eyes and took a deep breath to clear my head.

"Do tell, my dearest. What did you think hell was going to look like? Eternal punishment?"

"Pretty much. Screaming, suffering. The whole fire and brimstone thing, you know. Demons torturing the wicked in a variety of terrible ways." I admitted.

He laughed. "You've been misinformed. Stop reading those pretentious philosophical ramblings. I assure you, most of what you will read is authored by fanatics attempting to frighten people into submission. It is a common human theme."

Black retrieved a small box from an elegant chest. He opened it and smiled at the item within, then closed the box and brought it to me. He opened it again, showing me a beautiful pendant on a thin gold chain. The pendant was made of ivory upon which a whimsical looking snake had been carved.

"A souvenir of your visit," he said, closing the box and setting it beside my wine. "It's a poor likeness of your Felix, but I do hope you like it. It was carved for you in 1657. I had the mounting and chain added once I determine gold suited you best."

I assumed Hades had simply misspoken. As usual my assumption was wrong.

CHAPTER FOUR

Phantom of the Forest

t has been suggested the hardest part of jogging is putting on one's jogging shoes. For me the hardest part of jogging is jogging. But it was such a beautiful late summer morning even I could not waste it by going to the office. I drove to a spot in the Cleveland National Forest I had discovered just after the conference. The terrain was largely hilly so I figured it would be uncrowded unlike the level trails unserious joggers preferred.

The early morning air was warm with a lovely hint of moisture that was certain to disappear once the sun rose above the trees. And it was a luxury to be alone in a beautiful space. I will never understand the human preference for the clutter and congestion of cities to the exquisite expanse of nature.

As I expected, my only companions on the jogging path were a few squirrels dashing about and chattering at my intrusion. I chose a lazy trot to make my way through the groves of oaks and eucalyptus until pines began to replace them. The sound of birds blending with the crunch of my footfalls was nearly hypnotic.

My takeaway from the conference had narrowed down to two things. First, I will not have an affair with Mr. Black. I am not sure the suave, self-assured, CEO of the underworld is what he seems. He implied having memories of me from a time before I existed, or remember existing. As seductions go, his I-have-a-secret approach was as novel as it was utterly ridiculous. Besides he has not called in weeks.

Second, there is a disturbance in the system and the malfunctions are of concern to whoever is in charge. I am merely a cog in the system so I will leave the worrying to the undefined *them* of Betz's conspiracy theories which means keeping my distance from Mr. Black. Some cataclysm may be coming. From what I have learned, there is always a disaster in the offing for humanity. I knew I would be busy, but assuming I'm immortal, I also assume I will not be otherwise impacted.

Stopping to shake a pebble from my shoe, I rewound those assumptions. If two assumptions are both wrong, is it a double negative? Which would make the assumptions accurate, right?

I was standing there trying to untwist my tortured logic when a gust of cool air swept past me chilling the sweat on my skin and making me shiver. Looking around for the cause, I spied a figure perched on a large, shaded rock not far from the path.

He made no movement until I acknowledged him with a friendly wave. He beckoned me join him and, sensing a curious vibe, I stepped forward only to discover as I closed the distance between us, the man was newly dead.

"Wow, you can actually see me," he called out, getting to his transparent feet.

I checked my plaz. It was blank. Whoever this soul was, he was not assigned to me. I stopped walking, leaving a cautious distance between us. "I can see right through you as a matter of fact."

"How?" he voiced the very question I was pondering. "I mean, no one else seems to see me."

The phrase "I see dead people" came to mind, but I simply shrugged. "It's a puzzle to me unless you are dead. You realize you are dead, don't you?"

"Shit yeah!" He scowled. "Figured that out right away. This guy took me to some old resort or something with a huge steel gate all lit up in green and left me there. Next thing I know, I'm told they are closed and my guide is nowhere to be seen."

"What do you mean, they were closed?" Such a thing was impossible. As far as I knew, green gates were always open. The dude had to be color blind. But what he said next sent a shock through my system.

"Not closed exactly," he corrected. "They said there was no more room."

Impossible. I checked my wrist again. It was as dead as the man I was talking with. Then I remembered there were a lot of new reapers. One of them must have made a mistake, taken the guy to the wrong drop off.

"How did you end up here?" I asked.

The guy returned to his perch on the rock. "It's the funniest thing. I waited around for a while thinking they were on a break or something, but nothing happened. Then I was thinking of this place and suddenly I was just here."

His explanation felt like an aftershock. What he was saying was impossible unless one believes those ridiculous ghost stories humans love to scare themselves with. My brain felt like it needed a reboot. "Wait . . . wait . . . wait. You thought yourself here?"

"Yes, ah, no. I don't know," he slouched. "I tried thinking about heaven, but I didn't go there. Just here. This is nice but it isn't heaven, is it?"

I had no idea how to answer. Hell and heaven were amorphous terms not precise addresses as far as I understood. I found it annoying this fellow had more experience of the afterlife than I had.

"Best I can do is take you back to . . . "

He jumped up. "I told you its closed."

I forced myself to remain calm. The last thing this guy needed was another inept reaper. "All right. Then tell me about your life and how you died." Maybe I could figure out where he should be.

"I had a great life, except for the last few years." He settled back against the rocky outcrop. Apparently enjoying the opportunity to talk about himself, he rambled on until he finally got to something interesting. "I got into money trouble and my employer wouldn't help me out. Ya know, give me an advance or a loan or something. I had been with the bastard for six years and he won't even give me a damn advance. Spent all night hating on him. This morning, I tracked him to where he likes to camp and . . ." He ran spectral fingers through his spectral hair. "We argued. I . . . um."

"You killed him." Had to be. I could smell the guilt all over him.

The guy spun about and growled. "Yes, I shot him. So, what? He was a selfish jerk. Listen, this is bogus. What you gonna do? Arrest me?" He laughed. "I mean, like, what are you anyway, some sort of robot, or one of them Viking chicks? "

"I'm not a Valkyrie." At least I did not think so. Of course, our jobs are similar. The idea I was a robot was too insulting for a response.

"Whatever, bitch. If you know so damn much, then just take me to heaven. Now!"

I folded my arms and glared at him. "I'd say heaven is in the rear-view mirror. But I'll gladly take you back to the gate you spoke of."

The apparition snarled, shifting his appearance into a dark, malicious form. Then he disappeared. Just blinked out.

"Are you magic?"

A little girl peeked from behind a tree a few yards away. She stepped away from her hiding place and ran to me wrapping her arms around my legs.

"No. I am not magic. Are you?" I answered, putting my hand on her shoulder to verify she was not another specter.

She peered up at me with huge blue eyes. "Then how did you make the bad man go away?"

"You saw him?" I asked, shock number three skittering down my spine. The child was about five years old, I guessed, and it was obvious she had been crying. Her dress was torn and she must have been crawling through the forest for some time. I knelt to speak with her face to face.

"Yes, I've been following him," she admitted. "He is the man who hurt my daddy. He was yelling at Daddy."

I hugged her closer, getting a fuller story from her mind; surprised to discover the child had heard two gunshots. "I'm sorry that happened."

"Me, too." She looked up at me again. "Daddy told me to run, so I did. I saw you talking to the bad man. He looks kinda funny now, but I know its him." A tear made its way down her cheek. "I wish you were magic. Can you fix my daddy anyway?"

That was an interesting question. There was nothing on my plaz about either the killer or the victim. All I could think of to do was help the girl. "Let's see if we can find your daddy."

She took my hand and led me down the jogging path while my brain sorted out the chronology. I wondered if Betz knew what to do about the missing reaper and the 'free' spirit who was a killer.

Could he also be a suicide? He never said how he died. Would I find a reaper with the girl's father? So many questions and my plaz was no help whatsoever. I do not get paid enough for this, I told myself. I decided to just go along and find someone to take care of the little girl.

We left the trail and walked through the brush for a few yards then came to a clearing. The girl's father was sitting against a tree. There was a large bloodstain spreading at his shoulder, but he was clearly alive. I checked the bullet wound as he clasped the little girl to him. It was a small-caliber injury, through and through. He had called the ranger station and I could hear vehicles approaching.

I sat on the ground and held the child on my lap as the EMTs worked. He was going to be all right, I assured her. Everything was going to be fine. But I did not believe it. A closed gate. A disembodied soul wandering the forest. The system was definitely not all right. There was undeniably a disturbance in the force.

Once the authorities took the child and her father back to civilization, I answered a few questions about the "man" I had seen without mentioning he had transitioned. I had no doubt they would find a body nearby. And I decided not to mention the encounter to anyone. I would type no message on my plaz or confide the event with either Elly or Betz. It never happened. I can erase memories too, I decided. At the very least, I can keep this one to myself.

I went home, changed, and went into the office for the afternoon where I could spend a few peaceful hours sitting in my chair watching the dust motes drifting in the sunlight.

News was hardly better from the human perspective. Liz was occupied with a TV program describing the several most likely ways in which Earth would be destroyed. Evidently with no current catastrophe available, Liz was content to feed her obsession with a documentary so long as the Takis held out.

I tiptoed past, silently slipping into my office and shut out the world for what I anticipated would be hours of blissful nothingness. I got six minutes. Liz strolled in with the day's agenda. I scratched out all the items and handed the document back to her. She refused to accept it.

"It is not wise to put things off, boss. You never know when something terrible will happen. And then what have you got? Hum? Unfulfilled obligations."

IRS events were secondary to my real obligations, I thought. But to please her, I reinstated a phone call scheduled for three o'clock.

"Thank you." Liz rubbed her face, leaving a Taki powder fingerprint on her chin. "Now if a meteor should hit us at least you will be in good stead with the powers that be."

I laughed.

"It could happen, Missie. There are a million rocks up there. Who's to say which one has our names on it?"

Who indeed. And who is to say if the messenger of such gods could not possibly be a middle-aged human with an orange smudge on her chin?

I stopped by Tito's for dinner intending to dispel my malaise with a plate of scrumptious tacos. The place was empty even at the usually packed dinner hour and Darcy sat with me while her uncle prepared my dinner.

She looked tired, that bone-weary kind of tired I had no trouble relating to. I swept my hand across the table pretending to be brushing away crumbs and touched her finger. Her thoughts poured into my mind providing the source of the young woman's dismay. Her uncle was being harassed by a gang of thugs demanding a percentage of his business. I suspected they were more interested in the drug dealing than the bar, but Darcy appeared not to have put that together yet.

Three wanna-be gangsters had staked out a position across from Tito's and had been rousting customers when they exited the bar. Business was down by two-thirds and Darcy was extremely worried.

"Have you thought about my suggestion? I think you'd do better working at the IRS." I asked, wiping the condensation from an ice-cold glass of beer.

Darcy shook her head. "No, no. I cannot desert my uncle especially with all this trouble. I know he is not a good man, Miss Gwyn. But he takes care of me."

It was the first time she had indicated any possibility of the man's side gig. Searching her thoughts, I found no evidence she knew very much. I wanted to tell her the details of Tito's drug dealing and worse. Sometimes a moment happens when one can, in the words of Robert Frost, take "the road less traveled by" and change the course of a person's life. Would it help to tell Darcy why she had to get out? Or would it only reinforce her decision to help her uncle? I assumed just keeping an eye on the vulnerable young woman would be sufficient. It was an assumption that once again would prove incorrect.

My dinner was served just as my plaz notified me of a new assignment. Darcy packed the food to go and I chugged half the beer and left. Grabbing my cloak, I followed directions to a small house several blocks from my apartment.

Hood up, I entered the premises and made my way to a room at the rear. The name Millie Maise replaced the digits on my wrist. The name fit the elderly woman who lay beneath a knitted spread. Her peaceful face was framed by strands of long white hair. And she looked toward me with whited eyes but made not a sound.

Since she knew I was there, I lowered my hood and approached the bed. I touched her arm and she smiled. I could sense her fragile heartbeat and the peace with which she had accepted she was dying. There was no pain, no regret, only peace. Millie had been an artist. The walls of her bedroom were filled with portraits of those she loved enough to paint. Parents, children, friends, and lovers all rendered in moments of joy or pride at some accomplishment. They were with her in the room as they were vividly in her thoughts.

I sat with Millie until her spirit freed itself from her body. In spirit form, Millie was glorious. A lithe young woman with wavy red hair and bright blue eyes that smiled happily. We took our time going to the portal. Millie embraced the beauty of the world she had not seen clearly for a decade. Her artist eyes relished the landscape and embraced the faces of people who were going about their lives oblivious to us. To Millie it was her final portrait. The dead observing the living.

Reaping is a function I have performed many times. None have been as moving as the transition of Millie Maise. Each time I am fascinated by the thoughts, regrets, and fears of the person who is dying. How could one not be intrigued? I am a reaper. I am the one present at the most important event a human will experience.

The transition of Millie Maise was unlike any I had previously experienced. It was like a Norman Rockwell painting of the way things should be and a blaring reminder that things were not that way. True to the pathology of opposite day, the peace of Millie's passing did not penetrate through the frustrations of my day. I walked home growing angrier with each step. Angry at the would-be killer who had offed himself after terrifying a little girl. Angry at the system that could not get its act together. Angry at humanity for its inability to rise above its baser nature. Angry even at Darcy for not seeing what was right in front her. Angry at a universe that had stolen my memories.

I rounded a corner and saw the thugs who were threatening Darcy and her uncle. They greeted me with whistles and catcalls. I punched the first one in the face sending him to the pavement. Then I kicked the second man in the groin and watched the third goon back away. I flipped up the hood of my cloak and laughed as the delinquents shrieked at my disappearance.

When I finally made it home that night the phone was ringing. I tossed my briefcase to the sofa and hurried to the antique phone threatening to jump out of the drawer. I bumped my shin and cursed as I grabbed for the receiver, expecting to find some salesman who was going to get a string of expletives for my trouble.

"Whoever you are, go fuck yourself!" I suggested by way of answering.

"Good grief, Gwyn. Ever heard of phone etiquette?" Elly asked. "Bad day at the office?"

I rubbed my shin and took a deep breath. "This stupid phone. Have you and Betz abandoned the normal communication device on purpose? I mean, really, this device is ridiculous. At least buy a cell phone or something."

"Hang on a minute, will you?" Elly interrupted my tirade. "Cell phones can be hacked and who knows who's listening to all those conversations bouncing off the towers. Landlines are safer."

"Not you too. I can't deal with two episodes of the unexplained in one day." I almost hung up but my only other real friend was a snake and reapers can hold a grudge.

"Ooh, that sounds interesting. Do tell." Elly taunted me with the smug chuckle she had perfected.

"Do yourself a favor and don't ask. Besides, I fixed it. Everything is cool." I sank into a chair and hitched my aching leg over the plush arm. If only snakes could pour a glass of wine. Felix curled up on a nearby table and stuck his tongue out at me.

"Listen, Gwyn, I need a favor."

"Something illegal, I assume, considering your reluctance to use the quicker and I might add less painful plaz." My leg was still throbbing.

"Funny you should mention illegal." Elly sighed. "I'm in jail."

"Jail!" I jumped twisting my sore leg. "Ouch, damn it."

"It's not painful, Gwyn." she chuckled. "It's all a slight misunderstanding. But I need you to come bail me out."

"What jail?" I asked sounding calmer than I felt.

"I don't exactly know." Elly chuckled again. "Whatever jail they put thieves in."

"That would be all of them," I informed her. "What did you thieve, ah, steal?"

"Evidently I stole a car."

"Whose car?"

I could hear her talking with someone in the background. The urge to put the phone down and go grab a bottle of wine was almost overwhelming. Before I could, Elly came back with an answer.

"An alderman's car. A really nice SUV with GPS, leather seats and Sirius and . . . and a briefcase full of money in the trunk."

"Shut up, Elly." I held the receiver to my chest and sighed. If I ever write my autobiography there will be a chapter entitled Saint for a Day. This day. It has already made it to number three on my list of terrible days and was heading to number two if things went where I suspected Elly was taking it.

"Gwyn, listen. I need you to come get me. I do not know how to make bail. And I do not want to use my plaz. If I do, everyone, and I mean everyone, will know."

I laughed out loud. Reapers have many skills but maintaining a secret among themselves was not one. The money was no problem, but I needed to know where she was. And thinking of needs, I had a few myself. I needed new friends, a vacation and wine. Just a simple glass of wine.

"Okay, Elly. Ask the nice policeman where you are. I will come get you. Bail money in tow."

"Brilliant! You're a genius, Gwyn."

She gave me the address and I typed them into my GPS. She was four hours away. I could easily make it there before court would open in the morning. I took a shower, put on jeans and a sweatshirt, and took the time to look up the alderman she had mentioned.

ALDERMAN JANE BLANKENSHIP, UNMARRIED,
38, COMMUNITY ADVOCATE
FUNDED WOMAN'S SHELTER, ESTABLISHED MEDICAL
CLINIC AND HOUSING FOR HOMELESS PERSONS

The alderman sounded like a philanthropist. It was the final word on the readout that explained why Elly would have been involved with Ms. Blankenship, but not why Elly had stolen the woman's car.

DECEASED.

My car purred along the I-10 free of daytime traffic. Liz once told me music soothes the savage beast and my mood was close enough to that title. I dialed a radio station playing oldies and added my contralto to the Righteous Brothers, letting slide the incongruity of the fact I knew the lyrics while having no memory of how I had learned them. I kept the windows up. Reapers do not come with musical talents as standard issue. My job is to gather souls, not torture them.

By the third hour, I found myself bored with singing and turned off the music which gave an opening for my thoughts to produce a slew of questions. Why would Elly steal a car? What was up with a case of money in the vehicle? Was the alderman a crook?

I arrived in time to attend the court hearing and paid Elly's bail. Elly used the opportunity to fill in the details of her experience.

"I was on assignment to gather the alderman before she could accept a bribe." Elly informed me. If the bribe was completed, it would change the woman's afterlife.

"The plaz told you that?" I asked incredulous.

"Knocked my socks off, too." she admitted. "I've never had an assignment with instructions before. It's always been just name, place and time."

I nodded. "Mine, too."

"Well, I do serve a better clientele than you, but still," Elly shook her head. "Anyway, I blew it. I got there a little late. I saw her put something in the trunk then walk around and get behind the wheel. That was when she got shot."

"Shot dead?"

"Right through her temple. I pulled her body out of the car and told her soul to get into the passenger seat. She was highly agitated. I thought she might bolt, but she did what I told her. My plaz was going crazy. It kept streaking out and changing the drop off point. Like maybe she was not supposed to die. Or maybe taking the bribe money changed everything. I heard sirens coming and I, well, I just drove off."

This was so far beyond my experience I was fascinated. "Did you make it to the portal?"

"Yes."

"Did they take her?"

Elly looked at me like I had suddenly gone crazy. "What? Of course, they did."

I swung by my office after depositing Elly at her palatial home north of the city. Still dressed in the jeans and sweatshirt, I walked in at 3:30 p.m. in the afternoon and found my assistant Liz humming while she sorted through piles of folders and pink notes. I marveled at had how efficiently and cheerfully she worked. Beneath the formidable exterior, Liz was a very likeable individual. Organized to a fault, Liz was the agent I should have been.

She turned and greeted me with a smile despite my inappropriate attire. "Look what the cat finally dragged in!" she chuckled, hands on her hips in fake disapproval. "It's a good thing I don't worry about you. Otherwise, I might spend my days wondering what my boss was up to."

"A very good thing." I agreed, it struck me I took her for granted way too often, I walked to her desk and set down a cup of hot chocolate I had gotten in the lobby. Liz looked up from her work.

"What's that?" she asked. "Doesn't smell like coffee."

"Its hot chocolate. It's for you."

Liz's eyebrows lifted. "Really? My goodness, thank you."

"Actually, I'm thanking you for keeping this place functioning the way you do. I don't think I thank you enough."

I smiled when she blinked a bit confused. I had not brought her anything before. Nor had I looked at her, really looked at her to see the woman within. I saw tiny creases at her eyes. The edges of her mouth were tensed downward and her shoulders sagged wearily. I had always considered my assistant to be indestructible, but she wasn't. Her husband had died years earlier and her children were grown and gone.

Liz removed the cover and tasted the hot chocolate. "Umm, just the way I like it. How did you. . "

"Know you like extra whipped cream?" I completed the question. "Lucky guess." Not to mention the occasional odd stain on her ample bosom.

Liz set the chocolate on the console behind her, safely out of harm's way. "Don't want you to take it back when you see how much work remains to be done. The extensions are coming due like mad and it is playing havoc with your schedule."

She lifted a huge stack of files. "These are the very urgent ones," she grimaced. "Those over there are merely urgent."

My gaze traveled to a second pile on her desk. "I should have put some Bailey's in that hot chocolate." I quipped.

"Yes, you should have." She laughed, handing me a pile of folders.

I took the very urgent pile to my office. After a dozen calls and as many messages left, I did some creative payment planning and cleared a ton of calculating from my schedule. Every case got a generous settlement offered. Even cases I extended for the nth time got the kind of mercy I would have rejected out of hand days before. Not because the thought of impending disaster softened my heart. I had no such heart. What I did have was the sense that all else had become trivial.

Just before closing time, I buzzed Liz to see if she was willing to work late if I sprung for dinner. I had curry in mind. Liz told me she had sworn off curry. We compromised on Chinese and I placed a generous order despite Liz's insistence it was her job. The food arrived half an hour later and I invited Liz to join me in my office to eat.

"Where were you today, Gwyn?" she asked, scooping a large portion of lemon chicken to her plate. "Out somewhere thinking about how to motivate your assistant?"

"No," I chuckled. "I just needed a day. Went for a jog in the forest, then a drive and then another drive. It gave me time to think about the people I know. I realized what a treasure you are."

"Posh!" she scoffed, a bit of sauce on her chin. But I could see she was pleased.

CHAPTER FIVE

If You Are Going Through Hell, Move Quickly

t was unquestionably a black-eye. Recently inflicted by the look of it. The area around the eye had bloomed a sickly violet and a bit of residual swelling distorted the bridge of Darcy's nose. The assailant had been right-handed.

"Nice shiner!" I offered sympathetically when Darcy avoided looking at me while she set a glass of Guinness on the table.

"Thanks," she blushed. "I . . . I, um, did it on a cabinet door in the back."

People who cannot lie well just should not lie at all. She bent forward and began wiping my table with a clean rag. She was rubbing so hard I wondered if the lacquered finish was being removed.

"Don't be embarrassed, Darcy. I think the eye makes you look interesting. And I'll bet the drunks won't be messing with you for a while."

"You really think so?"

"No question about it. Everyone will be wondering what the other guy looks like." I lied with a smile and took a sip of beer. I did not need to touch Darcy to know what had happened. I could sense the hurt coursing through her. Uncle Tito had happened. Like usual, my assumption was wrong.

She stuffed the towel in her waistband. Looking at me directly for the first time, she managed a smile. "Can I ask you what that is on your wrist?"

I tapped my plaz to bring up the time on the screen.

"A watch!" she looked closely at the glowing numbers. "That's so cool. I thought it was a tattoo or something when I first noticed it."

"Do you like tattoos?" I asked tapping the plaz again to clear it.

"Not really. Some are pretty." Darcy fidgeted with her apron string. "But I don't know any nice people who have them. I was kinda hoping yours wasn't a tattoo."

I laughed. "Some ink is quite beautiful, but I know what you mean. Gangs use tattoos to mark their members." And there was Betz who seemed to bloom with new ink every time I saw her. But I doubted Darcy would know what to make of her.

Darcy paled for a moment then blurted out what was really on her mind.

"You remember those men I told you about? The ones who were bothering my uncle? They got attacked the other night. A woman beat them up," she studied my reaction. "A small woman with blonde hair. She was wearing a black cloak . . . like the one I've seen you in."

Busted. There was no point denying it, even if I wanted to.

"It was me if that's what you're implying," I admitted. "I'd hardly call it a beat down. They confronted me late at night and said the vilest things. I punched one and kicked the others so I could get away. Must have caught them by surprise."

Darcy sighed in what I took as a moment of relief. "The surprise was the way you disappeared," she said.

Truth only gets one so far, I decided. "And you believed them?"

She looked down at the floor. "No, not really. I mean who would believe something like that," she was practically whispering. "I laughed at them and called them cobardes . . . cowards." My uncle yelled silencio! Then one of the men hit me.

It was at this moment the idea to rescue Darcy took residence in my head.

Stepping out of the bar, I watched a Bentley pull to the curb in front of me. The enormous car looked like a battleship compared to the jalopies parked along the street. It was steel gray, polished to glossy perfection and instantly drew a crowd. Evidently even thugs get star struck. Cell phones recorded every inch of the car until a blast of hot wind moved people back clearing a path for me. I was hardly surprised when the rear window slid down revealing a familiar face.

"Need a ride?" Mr. Black queried cheerfully.

"I live two blocks from here, Black. I think I can manage it. Thanks anyway."

The chauffer alighted from the vehicle and rounded the rear of the car to open the door for me. I did a double take when he turned to motion me inside. His face was covered in thick brown hair that covered a canine snout complete with mustache and beard. He wore a dark uniform and a chauffer's cap set between elevated ears.

Mr. Black patted the seat beside him. "Come, Gwendolyn. It is far safer than trusting the sidewalks in this part of the city. I promise I won't bite." He chuckled when I nodded at the driver. "Neither will Louis."

I inched past the driver and settled into the seat across from Mr. Black who waggled his finger at me.

"Surely, you're familiar with lycanthropes," he remarked in that way he had of using a statement as a question.

"I have only read about them. Mainly stories about werewolves killing people in France years ago." I whispered.

"Ah, yes. The infamous werewolf terror known as the Beast of Gevaudan. 1765, I believe." He paused for a moment as if pulling up a specific memory. "Or are you referring to the French loup-garou epidemic in the sixteenth century? Entertaining episodes in either case."

The chauffer straightened his back and turned to me. "It is a pleasure to meet you, Miss," he growled, tipping his hat slightly.

Mr. Black motioned for Louis to proceed. "S'il te plait emmene nous au parc, Louie."

I settled back into my seat and watched the scenery pass; confident Mr. Black would get to the purpose of his visit. I had to admit I was pleased to see him. I hoped to pry more information about the coming catastrophe. Liz was winning me over and I was rattled by the weird snafus of the past few weeks. Black was obviously aware of my interest and politely left me to gather my thoughts. By the time we reached our destination, I had reduced my curiosity to a single query.

"What is happening?"

Mr. Black took a deep breath. "That is the question, isn't it."

We left the car and ambled through the park. Louie pulled out a turkey leg to munch on while he waited. Mr. Black, always one for maximum drama, threw his arms wide to embrace the lush foliage and sweet autumn fragrances so different from his own realm.

"I'm not entirely certain.," he said at last. "I share your curiosity, my dear. I have used my resources to seek the answer.

Alas, with no success. I do not even know from whom the information came. But it is genuine. Things are changing. All things change and not always for the better. Just look at how Gaia is changing life all around us even now."

"You must know more than you've told us. The end of the world would seem more newsworthy than a change of seasons." I half-joked.

Mr. Black stopped walking and shrugged. "That is a rather morbid conclusion, don't you think?"

"Then it is not the end of the world?"

"Perhaps the end of someone's world, Gwyn. The end of the world is a personal experience, not a universal one. We just went through a costly training. It would have been pointless to have done so if there was to be no need for reapers in the future."

"There'd be no further need for gods either," I pointed out as we found a bench.

"Not for gods. That is correct." He gave me a charming smile. "I am not a god, Gwyn."

"Then what is coming must be strictly about the humans." I surmised.

Black cleared his throat. "There are more things—than are dreamt of in human philosophy, to misquote Shakespeare. The difficulty here is human beings cannot grasp the existence of any species greater than themselves."

"Yet, here we are." I noted. "Maybe it is time humanity knew that."

It was the first time I heard Mr. Black laugh in complete and utter merriment. "Humanity does not want to know. They keep the secret from themselves."

"Then let's just tell them and be done with all these silly rules." I suggested earning a second laugh from him.

"Dearest Gwyn, I find your companionship delightful," he said in his most velvet tone of voice. "I always have."

He lifted my hand to his lips and I felt myself smiling despite all I knew. Or perhaps because of all the things I did not know.

"Enough, Hades," I purposely called him by the ancient name. "You have alluded to a past between us several times. But I have no memory of one."

Mr. Black stared at me; the strength of his gaze sufficient to freeze me in time. He knew! He knew why I had no memory. He knew about a past, now erased, that left me hollow. I could see him toy with the idea of giving me what I needed to know. Then he blinked.

"What are memories, Gwyn? Wishes that should have been fulfilled so we convince ourselves they were?"

"I have no memories so I cannot answer that. Only you can!" I let my disappointment come through in my voice. He rocked back putting a bit of distance between us.

"It is best for you to accept your situation, Gwyn. Think of it as a blessing that spared you from a worse fate." He reached up and ran a finger along my cheek "If you want memories, I am more than willing to create new ones with you."

I turned away and saw Louis approaching. I fixed my attention on him. Did humans see the werewolf, I wondered. I did, I saw the wolf and more. I saw the gentle man within him.

"Ah, Louie, has my call come through?" Mr. Black asked as the chauffer joined us and handed his boss a cell phone. He looked at me and sighed. "Pity, alas, the timing is poor."

"Every day contains a new experience. I think that is considered a curse in some cultures. Not that I can remember which ones." I said as Black walked away to take his call.

Louis smiled. "Are you keeping up with your reading? The past is all there if you dare to see it." He chuckled. "You must have patience, Gwyn. Even Felix knows that."

Mr. Black met us at the car. He told Louis to get ready to leave and took my hand. "I'm dreadfully sorry, Gwyn." There was a deep concern on his face. "I must leave immediately. Can we drop you off at your apartment?"

"No. The walk will do me good."

"Be safe. I have taken care of those punks who bothered you the other night. But there are always others willing to harm you."

I lingered in the park watching the sun set and waiting for the denizens of the night to emerge. Fairies tended to the flora. Their little hands caressing leaves and repairing wounds caused by human feet during the day. I watched them groom the trees and shrubs and listened to their whistles and laughter. The air filled with their scent, honey and mint that soothed the soul.

When I finally returned to my apartment, Felix was on the kitchen counter waiting for me to tend to him. He lifted his head and flicked his tongue welcoming me home. I gave his head a gentle pat. Digging out a thawed mouse, I watched him take it and settle down to consume his meal. Felix was a lesson in getting what he needed. Maybe that is what Louis had meant. He was patient and a good listener. He concealed his emotions and was rewarded in the end with what he wanted.

"We have to talk," I told him.

A snake of quiet contemplation, Felix did not respond. But I wanted his approval and knew he was a good listener. I leaned back against the counter and folded my arms.

"Do you remember when we met? You were in the window of the reptile store on Adams. It was the day after I had awakened and I was walking around getting familiar with my surroundings. I stopped to watch you and you lifted your head to stare right back at me. You were so beautiful, and there was an intelligence in your eyes so different from the dull look of humans. Most of them anyway. I knew I had to free you."

Felix flicked his tongue and slithered over to me and put his head on my arm.

"You were my first purchase, my first friend. I think it will be same with Darcy. I am going to set her free too."

My plaz alerted me at 9:47 p.m. with an assignment. I had drifted off and responded to the plaz with a disoriented rereading of the information. There were three names.

"Oh goodie, a threesome," I muttered making my way to the closet. "Give me a minute, boys."

Half an hour later, expecting to find the aftermath of a gang dispute, I was surprised to discover a plane crashed in the middle of nowhere. The private jet had flown into the side of a rather low hill. Firemen were on scene dousing the scruffy brush around the site and ambulances were arriving to remove the victims. I saw there were five victims in total, three of which were assigned to me.

"How are you doing, Gwyn?" a voice inquired from behind me. The speaker was Drake whom I had met at the coven. Drake was eager to tell me what had occurred.

The plane had been chartered by a cartel leader who was enroute to inspect the operations of a new business he had started.

The operation provided a dark net site for a particularly disgusting brand of pornography and the cartel had provided not only money but unwilling actors.

"I am here for the girlfriends," Drake informed me. "You've got the pilot, the cartel guy, and the bagman. I could have handled it all, but there may be an issue with the portals. My usual one went yellow yesterday." He shrugged. "Those work sessions were worth it, don't you think? It's been weird ever since."

I nodded. "I've noticed."

A pair of spirits began to rise from the crushed remains of the Cessna tail section. Drake left to claim his assigned specters, two females who floated over to him yelling like they were annoyed at the service. Drake lassoed the ladies and led them away.

My assignments took a while. The pilot was loaded into an ambulance and was being worked on in a futile attempt to save the guy. The bag man was trapped in the wreckage and rescuers were not going to reach him before he transitioned given the sound of his heartbeat. The essence of the cartel boss was waiting a distance away. He had covered his spectral ears to blot out the noisy females. He was cursing when I approached him attempting to convince me it was a mistake and he could not possibly be dead. I let him rant until the other two specters joined us then led them to the unanticipated end of their journey.

Later that day, I was sitting at my desk watching sunlight flowing through slats in the window shade, when Elly burst into my office. My harried secretary was chasing after her.

"Hey, lady, you can't go in . . . Liz barked barely escaping being clocked by the door Elly slammed behind her.

"Got your cloak?" Elly winked at me; a bit breathless after running up the stairs.

I nodded at my coat rack.

Liz reopened the office door and was about to lay hands on Elly when I waved her away. "It's okay, Liz," I assured my assistant and watched disappointment cloud her face as she backed out and shut the door.

Elly gave me a mischievous grin. "Then grab it and let's go. I have a cab waiting."

She turned on her heel barely giving me time to grab the garment from my coat rack. We came within an inch of bowling Liz over when we opened the door she had been listening through. I gave her a shrug and followed Elly into the hall. I was happy for the distraction. Even ignoring my IRS workload had become boring and I was curious as to what Elly had in mind. Two thirty was well past lunch and too early for dinner.

Elly's sense of urgency had infected the cab driver who shot away from the curb the second we were seated and dove into traffic as if it did not exist. I observed the green glow from Elly's plaz and checked my own. It was dark. At least I had not missed some communal message.

"Where are we going?" I asked.

Elly chuckled. "You will see. It is a surprise."

I folded my cloak in my lap. "I hate surprises."

"No, you don't." Elly contradicted me. "Your entire life is a surprise. We never know when an assignment will be received or who our client is. Lately they have been coming rapid fire. I have one now and I wanted you to come with me."

"I don't classify an assignment as a surprise, Elly."

"I'd bet your clients do," Elly laughed.

We left the city behind and headed into the posh estates along Sky Ridge Hills. Mansion after mansion passed by as we made our way into the most expensive neighborhoods where mere mansions gave way to estates. I assumed Elly was just showing off. Here lived the modern robber barons of industry and finance. Even the air seemed rarified and our cabbie was wide-eyed as he negotiated the manicured roads.

He turned down a side street lined with cherry trees that fronted a high, tactfully obscured brick fence. Elly rechecked the address on her plaz then paid the cabbie who offered to wait for us as long as necessary. He obviously did not expect for us to be let into the estate much less last long inside.

"You sure you want me to leave you here, ladies?" he asked recounting the generous tip he had just received. "I can turn off the meter and wait right here. You wouldn't have to wait for another cab to get way out here, ya know."

He was more concerned another cabbie would get the next big tip. I scanned the landscape but found no sign of emergency vehicles or police. My plaz was still blank. A large house sat atop a rise. It was impressive looking and silent as death.

"Who died?" I asked once the cab had traveled out of sight.

Elly picked the lock on the huge wrought iron gate. "It is a mystery to me, too. I have not gotten a name yet. What do you say we go find out?"

We made our way up the gravel driveway then skirted the main building and detoured to a garage at the back. Bird calls and the occasional rustle of leaves were the only sounds. We donned our cloaks, using the hoods to make us invisible to human eyes. We found a gazebo nearby and decided to wait comfortably. Elly filled me in on the few details she had gathered. The estate belonged to Regina Pendleson, a well-known socialite from a family whose wealth went back to the era of the civil war. She was notoriously recluse and said to be stingy with her wealth, avoiding fundraisers like the plague.

"She has no such reticence when it comes to accepting awards," Elly noted. "And she rules her holdings with an iron fist. No one dares confront her. In fact, the only person to have penetrated her standoffish persona is her husband, Archibald Pendleson. They were married six months ago. He is said to be extremely handsome and ambitious. Rumor has it, Regina's money is what he covets, to get where he wants to go."

"Which is?"

"Dubai."

Archie has a lucrative business opportunity in the Middle East and once the deal was signed, he merely needed to discard his wife. It was a classic story and reapers were inevitably needed in the end.

"I found an online article by JB Morice; a real hit job on Regina." Elly continued. Morice got a fat bonus for writing it. She is a gossip more than a journalist and Regina Pendleson is hardly her first victim. I half expect to see Morice's name on my plaz."

My head was spinning. "Archie stole not only Regina's heart but her money. Looks to me like Archie's your assignment."

"Might as well throw in the wife. The way I heard it, revenge is Regina's middle name. I would not be surprised if she got the writer fired."

I chuckled. "I see why you brought me along. Whichever one of them kicks the golden bucket is going to be pretty angry. Care to wager dinner on who the loser is?"

"There's enough greed and duplicity going on here to choke a politician," Elly laughed. "Isn't it fabulous? I cannot wait to see how it ends. I thought you would find it amusing and it does you good to get out of that hovel you live in."

The sound of footfalls coming from the gravel path made us turn our heads. We hurried to the side of the master house to see who was approaching.

"That is JB Morice. Her picture was attached to the article." Elly whispered. "What is she doing here? One would think this is the last place she would be." She glanced at her plaz and gasped. "I can't effing believe this." She showed me her plaz and I shook my head.

Archie was the first one out of the house to greet the reporter. We watched as he gave the woman a hug and pleaded with Morice to leave. But before the writer could, Regina stepped out and fired two bullets before raising the gun to her own head and firing a third.

"Well, you were correct about the surprise." I admitted.

Elly gathered the souls of the husband and wife while I tended to Morice. Touching her I got a rush of anger and betrayal from the journalist. Archie had manipulated the woman to write the vicious article. Promises were made. But JB discovered they were not going to be kept. She had come to confront Archie. Her last breath was filled with wrath. Yet another sin she will get to answer for.

Elly and I herded the trio to the assigned portal and left those on the other side to sort out what would become of them.

Felix was sitting on the ancient tome when I got home. It was a not-so-subtle plea for attention and I fell for it happily. A good story would reset the mood and push back thoughts of what had been a crazy day. Sitting beside Felix on the sofa, I paged through the parchment entries looking for a story that would entertain and found one titled *Dumbass of 1856*. Felix gave the pick a nod of approval.

"The coordinates directed me to a place near where I had been a decade earlier. This time, instead of a blizzard, I was traveling on a warm summer day which was a blessing in more ways than one. My previous visit involved victims of the wickedest winter weather the Sierra Nevada mountains could produce. It had been a pitiful scene. Whole families dead of starvation and subzero temperatures. I could feel grief still clinging to the trees even though much time had passed.

"I climbed high into rugged stone using the small plateaus to catch my breath and check my plaz. I could hear small animals scurrying in the thick brush and birds calling as they soared on the strong draft of wind butting into the vertical granite spires that soared ever upward. At last, I came to campsite tucked behind a wall of boulders larger than a cabin. A hovel fashioned of leafy branches was strung between two pines trees. A few feet away, a fire pit had grown cold and I wondered if my assignment had already died. Then I heard a puma scream and the sound of someone running. My plaz flashed, the transition was imminent.

"I found the man standing at the base of a ten-meter granite wall. At the top of the wall was a magnificent stag peering tensely at the man below and the mountain lion on a ledge above him. The human hunter was a man in his fifties. He was dressed in buckskin

trousers and a tattered vest. His hair and beard were matted, making it impossible to ascertain the color beyond a tan reminiscent of deer hide. He wore boots and a sidearm and carried a Winchester rifle which he cocked and raised to sight on the stag.

The animal reared up just as the man pulled the trigger and I saw the bullet tear a hole in the stag's muscular chest. Four hundred pounds of male deer stumbled forward and fell from the ledge, landing on the man with a sickening crunch. The lion crouched down and studied the carnage below. He cocked his head as if trying to decide which of the carcasses he preferred for his supper.

The dead hunter's spirit rose up slowly. He raised his arms then dropped them in disgust. I walked over and touched his shoulder.

"Now don't that beat all?" he asked shaking his head. "Damn cat is the winner. I been tracking the deer for three hours and the cat shows up to take the kill. I just wanted to beat him to it. What do you make of something like this here?"

"Karma," I said softly.

"What the hell is that?"

"Look it up. You'll find your image."

He gave me a confused look. "One of them tintype things? Did they put my name on it?"

"I think they just labeled it dumbass."

"He shook his head up and down. "Cannot fault 'em for that," he agreed following me as I led him to the portal."

CHAPTER SIX

Technical Difficulties

Oversleeping when your pet is a snake is a piece of cake when compared to having furry friends. Snakes cannot scamper across the duvet or jump off the headboard and land on your head. They do not growl or bark or lick you. What snakes do is quietly coil at your feet and stare at you with mysterious eyes.

Felix was wound around my feet, his head raised high enough to see my face. He flicked his tongue in a silent show of impatience.

I tossed back the covers and followed him into the kitchen. I microwaved a mouse popsicle and set it aside to cool. Never one to abide by rules or manners, Felix snapped it up immediately.

"Libertine!" I muttered leaving Felix to his morning meal.

I, on the other hand, thought myself a loyal adherent to the system that governed my existence. Even though ours was anything but a reciprocal relationship. The system was changing without so much as an if you please. Well, I did not please at being left in the dark, and there was no one for me to stare at. And to be honest, I was not certain of what I wanted. Other than something beyond a microwaved rodent.

A hot shower later, my outlook had improved. Somewhere between getting soap in my eyes and rinsing it out, I had a revelation. There was nothing I could do about my lost memory, or the turmoil everyone thought was coming. However, Darcy's plight was an issue I could do something about.

Giving my hair a cursory toweling, I went naked in search of my landline phone. It was the weekend, so Betz was probably available unless she was booked for some bachelor's party. Hoping my friend was free, I looked up her number and dialed the landline phone. Betz answered on the second ring.

"What do you do?" I laughed. "Sit by your phone all day?"

"Gwynie, it's so nice to hear from you," she replied more than a trace of sarcasm in her voice. "What's up? Did that reptile bite you? You sound kinda snakebit."

"Not at all. Felix enlightens me. And I would like to get your advice on something."

"O-h-h k-a-a-y," she drawled. "But I'm as green as you, Gwyn. No one has ever asked me for advice."

I set the receiver down and wrapped a fresh towel around me. "You ever tried to make something right? I mean you see a bad situation and decide to take action on your own."

"Nope. I usually get there early, watch the transition take place and drop the soul off at a portal. Never tried to intervene or anything. Firstly, I do not care that much about humans. Second, wasn't that covered at the conference?"

Given the quantity of alcohol Betz had imbibed at the conference, I was not surprised by her confusion.

"Which reminds me," she continued. "Are your portals acting strange? I had one shut down on me before I could dropkick the guy in. Embarrassing. I had to drag him half way across town to another one."

"Yeah, I have had that problem and worse. They warned us it might happen. Had that big chart of portals showing all the new ones."

Betz snorted. "Listen, pondering all that ephemeral shit at the conference about preparing for a catastrophe nobody can identify is a dead end. I mean, there aren't enough clues to conjure up a decent conspiracy. I hope you have one." Betz chuckled. "I love me a conspiracy."

"Not exactly," I told her. "But I do have a favor to ask if you are up to testing the limits."

"I'm game. Who do you want me to kill?"

"Funny you should say that, Betz," I chuckled. "There is this guy I've had my eye on . . . "

"Oh, Gwynie, you are making my day! For real? I have been wanting to take someone out since I learned reapers used to kill people, you know, in the past. Wow!" She practically squealed. "It will save so much time. And we could be avengers. I can't tell how often I've wanted to break some asshole's neck."

"Hold on, Betz. I just need a wing man."

"I'm in. I think it sounds delightful. But I prefer to be considered your coconspirator, okay? Wingman sounds so military. Not to mention it also misgenders me."

I rolled my eyes. "Okay, co-conspirator it is."

"Let's continue this discussion face to face, Gwyn. Meet me at the train station tonight at 8 p.m." Betz said then ended the call just as a low growl rattled the window. The room shook for a few seconds, jostling the furniture and disrupting the alignment of my reaper posters.

A hum rose from the street below where people stood frozen in place and gazed up at the taller buildings waiting for a bigger jolt that did not come.

Liz was engrossed watching an endless loop of images showing damage caused by a small earthquake. It is astonishing how interesting she found watching the same dishes fall from a cabinet or a stop sign swing from side to side.

"Those poor people," she said taking a piece of chocolate from a Hershey Bar. Evidently the Taki binge had run its course. Or perhaps, Liz selected a specific edible for each type of disaster. A point I decided not to ponder.

"I'm sure they all have insurance, Liz."

"You never know." She retorted. "Some people procrastinate about being prepared for earthquakes, or meteors, or . . ."

"A zombie apocalypse. Uh-huh," I grunted without noting aloud that Liz's personal disaster preparation consisted of nothing more than watching the news while consuming snacks.

Liz handed me a few pink slips regarding phone calls I had to return. "Have you noticed how many disasters there are lately? There was the hundred-year flood in China, the earthquake in Turkey, bird flu breakouts somewhere and God knows what else. It's getting down right biblical, well, except for here. Everything is fine here."

I could have mentioned the portal disruptions, but that would have blown her mind. "I will bring the wrath of God down on a few tax payers today, Liz. Does that count?"

"It will have to do," she chuckled.

I heard Liz cross over to the file cabinet and start mumbling under her breath.

"Tarnation!" she muttered loud enough for me to hear. "It's jammed."

"Give it a bash."

"I tried that," she insisted. "Probably got effected by the earthquake earlier."

I went over and shook the cabinet. The drawer remained stuck. "Is it unlocked?"

"Don't you go saying this is my fault, Missy. I unlock the cabinet every morning," she blew a strand of hair out of her eyes. "So, what do we do now?"

"Call maintenance." I told her returning to my desk.

"I would but I would probably be fired or get a verbal beating for bothering them." She yelled back.

I ordered curry for lunch and worked my way through the day despite my mind wanting to return to the issue of Darcy and her despicable uncle. My adrenalin was pumping and I stayed late getting close to caught up before grabbing a hot dog and ear of corn from a street vendor on my way to meet Betz.

I arrived at the train station three minutes earlier than the "always early" Betz who was half an hour late. We bought coffees and looked for a private space to talk. The station was crowded; more with homeless squatters than travelers. We decided to go sit in my car.

"Thanks for not blowing me off," I said once we got settled.

Betz smiled. "I'm curious. I mean I'm not surprised; you have a reputation for breaking the rules. Even if you act rather old school most of the time."

"I am not old school, Betz," I defended myself. "And I have never broken the rules. I didn't even know what they were before the conference."

"Sure. Is that why you're so uptight lately. You haven't slept with Blacky yet, have you!" she waggled her eyebrows. "You really should, you know. He's a hunk."

The leather seat squeaked as I squirmed uncomfortably. "No, but not because of any rule. I jus . . . "

"Because there is no rule about sex," Betz interrupted. "You just think it's inappropriate."

"I'm not interested in Mr. Black in that way!"

"He's obviously interested in you . . . that way." Her smile became a grin. "Shit, Gwyn, Blacky is gorgeous."

"Can we move on, please."

Betz finished her drink and set the empty cup in the holder. "You want to kill someone but you're uncomfortable talking about sex. If you asked me, a little horizontal mamba would do you a world of good."

"I know about sex, Betz. I have enough problems without worrying about my libido."

"You have to experience a subject to understand it."

I tossed the remnants of my coffee out the window. I was beginning to develop an experiential understanding of wrath. "Do you want to teach me about sex before we commit murder or after?" I jested.

Betz adjusted her seat and reclined in thought. "After. Definitely, after. When your juices are flowing and you're all pumped up."

My jaw dropped and Betz convulsed in laughter. I accepted the fact that planning an attack on Darcy's uncle was going to take much longer than I expected if my coconspirator was going to wander off on tangents. Attempting to return to the main topic, I explained the basics about Darcy and her unsavory uncle.

Betz listened politely. "Humans are fragile compared to other species, Gwyn. There are thousands of ways to kill them."

Mercifully Betz felt no need to list them all. "A good, swift clean murder would be best. We will just cut his throat."

The car started shaking as a new tremor passed through. I watched dust rise off the asphalt as Betz opened her car door.

"Just in case," she explained giving me an embarrassed grin. Neither of us were familiar with the science of tectonic movement. The quake stopped after a few seconds, and Betz leaned back into the car.

"I think we should put the Uncle Tito caper off for a day or two," she suggested. "Until these quakes stop. If a big one hits, we might have to harvest a lot of souls."

The worst thing I predicted was that Liz's cabinet would be jammed again. I found the word murder much more alarming than the idea of a big earthquake. We checked our wrists and parted ways.

Felix was unconcerned by either the quakes or my pending criminality. I hauled out the ancient tome but I was much too keyed for a story, deciding instead to merely chat with my pet. I climbed into bed and waited for him to settle on a nearby table.

"Louis knows about you, Felix. I don't suppose you could tell me how you met." I sighed. "He said we are going through, what did he call it? Difficult times and it's hard not to agree with . . ." The lights went out at that moment throwing the whole neighborhood in darkness. "See what I mean?"

I hunted for some candles and matches. Checked my plaz to see if it was affected and scrounged for something edible without being microwaved. I pulled out a frozen mouse to thaw. There was no reason for Felix to be inconvenienced if the outage lengthened into a few days.

I opened the window in the living room and was rewarded with a cool breeze laced with smoke. A group of teenagers had lit a trash can on fire across the street from the apartment. It cast an orange glow that shimmered in the dark. The boys were celebrating with a case of warm beer one of them had taken from an alley.

"Hey, Lady. You Gwyn?" One of the boys threw a pebble against the wall near my window.

"Yes." I answered curious how he got my name.

The boy lifted a small package. "Got a present for you. It's got your name on it. Gwyn Reaper. It was in your mail box. Apartment 310, right? Come on down and get it. Might even throw in a free beer, if you are nice."

His companions found that amusing.

I told him to put it back where he got it and the group laughed even harder. I watched them head toward the building entrance and I shut the window. Cursing when I heard them on the stairs I picked up Felix and draped him around my shoulders.

"It looks like Uncle Tito is not going to be the first villain to get kicked off the island, Felix. Let's see what they think about you."

There was a bang at the door. I waited for the second knock, opened it, and watched the reaction. The leader took a step forward coming face to face with my curious pet. Felix flicked his tongue and the boy tripped backward with a scream. His posse long gone, like his bravado, the boy dropped the box and fled. Felix slid down my leg and inspected the box. I retrieved them both and shut the door.

The return address was a single word: *anamnesis* remembered things from a previous existence. I removed the wrapping and found a small frame containing a painting of a young woman who looked exactly like me. Standing beside her was Mr. Black.

The next night, Betz arrived wearing black slacks, a black long-sleeved shirt and dark cap fully covering her short black hair. She also brought a mood bordering on exuberant.

"Good grief, Betz, you look like a cat burglar."

She stood in my doorway and leaned in to carefully survey the room. "Where is it?"

"I locked Felix in his cage," I assured her. "Just for you. He is going to pout for days. Come on in."

Betz took a cautious step forward enabling me to shut the door. She removed the knit cap and ran her fingers through her hair. "I like to be in character when I can," she said giving me a once over. "You're not seriously thinking of dressing like that, are you?"

"What's wrong with shorts and a shirt?" I demanded. "We'll be wearing our cloaks. I mean, Geezus, Betz."

"Do you dress like that for the office?"

"Of course, not. There is a dress code."

Betz plunked down into a chair. "Has it occurred to you there might be a dress code for criminals?" She said crossing her arms and giving me a "gotcha" look.

My eyes rolled, but to avoid an argument not worth having, I went and changed into dark clothes. Before leaving I flipped on the TV and set the volume just high enough for someone in the hallway to hear. As alibi's go, the noise and lights left on would make it possible for neighbors to believe I was home. A final bathroom visit, then we donned our cloaks and we set out for the bar.

It was a warm night but not oppressive. The day's heat still radiated up from the concrete sidewalk as we slipped into a series of alleyways. Betz took off her cloak and climbed over the piles of garbage strewn along the crumbled asphalt. I watched for strangers but the alley was too filthy for even the homeless to have taken refuge. On either side of us were the backs of small stores long since closed for the day or in some cases the decade.

Darcy's bar appeared like a freshly swept oasis amid a desert of trash. Boxes and abandoned vehicles formed a fence blocking the small patio on both sides. There was a chair and a table set beside the door which led into the rear of the bar and a single bulb served as guard, illuminating the small area with yellow light. We crouched behind a rusted Chevy sedan, sans tires, and settled in to wait for Tito to appear.

It wasn't long before a trio of men strolled out of the darkness on the opposite side of the patio and knocked four times on the bar's door. The door opened and the men went inside, quickly returning to the patio a few moments later and disappearing down the dark alley. Betz nudged me in the ribs.

"Did you see how they were dressed?" she whispered. "I told you. What were those men doing?"

"I don't know for sure, but the uncle must be a man of few words." I speculated. "Maybe they were picking something up?"

"Shhh!"

The back door opened again and Darcy stepped out. She tossed a bag of trash into a large metal container directly in front of the chevy carcass concealing us.

"Shit!" I had not expected Darcy to still be working. It was past midnight and she should have been long gone.

"Don't tell me that's the innocent young thing you are trying to save," Betz whispered. I could hear the amusement in her voice.

I nodded. Darcy had not been present the previous night when I had checked the place. There had only been a series of men coming and going in thirty-minute intervals. Even more disturbing than Darcy's presence was the way she was dressed. Not in waitress garb as I had always seen her, the young woman was wearing tall boots, a short skirt, and a pink tube top. The outfit added a page to her life story I had never read. It also confirmed a part of her uncle's nefarious business I had preferred only to suspect.

Darcy flipped the metal lid closed. It banged loudly echoing down the alley and causing Betz to startle. She bumped the Chevy with her knee and yelped. Darcy's head pivoted in our direction and her gaze swept across the Chevy. Betz and I ducked as low as possible. A moment later, we heard the back door open and shut.

It was then or never, I realized. We draped our cloaks over our shoulders and raised the hoods pulling them low on our brows making us invisible to anyone who might come by before I completed my task. On second thought, I removed my hood. I wanted Uncle Tito to see the reaper coming for him. We climbed around the Chevy, stepped onto the lighted patio, and gave each other a thumbs up. Betz settled into the chair beneath the yellow light. I turned the handle and opened the back door.

It opened to a small, dimly lit room. A heavy-set man was seated at a makeshift desk. Behind him was a shelf containing a dozen or so wrapped packages like the one the men had brought out with them earlier, each package bearing a slip of paper identifying either content or receiver. To his right was a stack of bins. Evidently the man was in the process of allocating his deadly merchandise to his minions. To his left was a door to the bar proper.

The man appeared to be in his fifties with longish dark hair and brown eyes. He wore a muscle shirt and was busy with the scale carefully measuring pills into small plastic packets. I stood silent by the door and waited for him to acknowledge me. When he did, his face twisted into a hideous grin.

"What the fuck are you?" he growled. His hand moved toward the gun on his desk, but he did not pick it up. Instead, he stood and moved from behind the desk to confront me.

I turned the cap on my cane to activate the blade and revealed my scythe. "I am here for you, Tito."

"I'm flattered," he chuckled. "But I am not available right now. Get your sorry ass out of here before I..."

His eyes widened. He reached back and turned the desk lamp toward me for a better look. Then recognizing the figure before him, the man made a strangled noise in his throat and backed away. He bumped against the desk, spilling pills everywhere and knocking his gun to the floor.

I stepped forward to close the distance between us and watched horror spread across his face. Raising my scythe, I swung it with all my strength intending to remove the man's head in a quick, fluid motion.

At that moment, the interior door shot open and Darcy stood in the doorway. I saw blood spray in front of me and caught Darcy opening her mouth to scream. She may have even begun the scream, but I did not hear it. A hand reached from behind me, and I heard fingers snap. An instant later, I was in my apartment, standing next to a disoriented Betz.

CHAPTER SEVEN

That Which Does Not Kill You, Disappoints Me

woke the next morning expecting to see police officers staring at me from the foot of my bed. Or a Dear Jane letter from Felix pinned to my pillow. Neither of those things occurred. Instead, I was greeted by a warm breeze wafting in from the window carrying the familiar signs of a typical fall morning on the street below.

Felix slithered to the top of my bedside table and appraised me, evidencing neither sympathy nor disdain. At least his tongue was not doing that impatient flicker Felix uses when he wants something. I took a breath and let it out slowly. Maybe it had been a bad dream. Or maybe I could make it through the day if I pretended Darcy had not seen me kill her uncle.

The ruse lasted just over an hour.

"Have you seen the news?" Liz asked, offering me a donut from the box on her desk.

My heart sank. And my stomach rejected the idea of eating out of hand.

"There was a train derailment near Temecula. Amtrak. The authorities are pulling survivors out just now. The video is wrenching." She stuffed half a donut in her mouth and mumbled. "Wanna hava rook?"

"Naw," I headed to my sanctum, chuckling. "The losses are deductible if Amtrak calls."

Liz trotted over to my door. "That reminds me. A Mr. Black called just before you got here. He has such a lovely voice. I didn't see him on the client list." She gave me a sideways glance. "He wouldn't be a special friend, would he?"

"No. Mr. Black is, well, Mr. Black." I told her. "Did he happen to leave a number?"

She dug into her pocket and pulled out a slip of paper. "Yes, here it is. I wrote it down in the call book too. Just in case you need it again." She smiled as if exceedingly pleased, then went back to her desk.

I poured a cup of coffee and played with the slip of paper while I drank. I decided to call Mr. Black later after my nerves had settled and Liz had gone to lunch. I tucked the paper in my drawer and told Liz to send my first client in when he arrived.

"He's already here," Liz said as she let a tall young man into my office and handed me the guy's file.

"You're not going to bust my balls, I hope," Mr. Jackson said as he took the lone chair in front of my desk. "I hear dealing with the IRS can be murder."

Is it written on my forehead, I wondered.

"Mr. Jackson, your balls are perfectly safe, I assure you." I gave him a half-hearted smile. "But your bank account may be in danger. It says here you owe several thousand dollars in taxes for the last three years. I can set up a payment plan, if you need one. In fact, this could all have been done over the phone if you had just called."

The man coughed. "I thought it would be better to come in person. You can see I am not rich. I live with my poor, sick mother and recently got laid off."

His eyes moved side to side as he talked. If I had a dollar for every time I'd heard a similar story, I could have bought an island. If the sob stories were true, the country would be populated by unemployed orphans. Still, there was something sincere about the guy's watery eyes. I handed him a tissue, making sure to touch his skin when he took it. Amazingly, Mr. Jackson was telling the truth. His mother was ill, he had very little money, and worked at a hardware store until last month when it went out of business. The money owed had accumulated over the years and was as much penalties as actual tax. I thanked him for coming in and told him I would erase the debt because he took the time to come in personally. He thanked me profusely. And I wished him luck.

I handed the folder to Liz, telling her to update the system and mark Mr. Jackson paid in full.

"We are not going to balance at the end of the month, if I do." She warned.

I sat on the edge of her desk and looked over at the scenes of wreckage on her TV. "Somebody's having a bad day," I pointed out. "What's the harm in balancing that out?"

"You are a softy; that's what you are!" Liz smiled. "I say may the Lord bless you for it."

She gathered the enormous tote bag she used for a purse, possibly a bug-out bag given her addiction to disasters, and headed out to lunch and a dental appointment, leaving me alone with a piece of paper containing Mr. Black's phone number.

I went to my desk and picked up the landline to return the call. Then, the door to my office flew open, and Darcy walked in.

"Darcy? How the hell, I mean . . . what are you doing here?"

She was dressed in a stylish black dress and heels. Yet another side of the young woman I had twice misjudged already. "You told me a while back you'd help me if I needed it. The bar is closed, and I have no money to open it again. My uncle . . . my uncle is . . ." She paused and studied my reaction.

"Of course, I'll do anything I can," I assured her, sounding sincere while my nerves were screaming *danger, danger*. In the best of outcomes, Darcy's arrival meant I could learn what precisely the young woman had seen in that split second when she had opened the door. Hopefully, she had registered very little other than the blur of her uncle being beheaded.

She took a seat opposite me and flashed a smile that never made it to her eyes. "You used to be my hero. You came in all the time with that friend of yours, looking all sophisticated and pleased with your pleasant, easy lives. And every time I saw you, I believed there was something better in life than what I was doing. Where I was. Last night I saw you for what you are. A murderer just like my uncle. Just like all the mean, stupid people in my horrible life."

I felt my heart racing at the disclosure. "What are you talking about, Darcy?"

"I saw you swing that big blade thing. I saw blood sprayed everywhere, and my uncle fell to the floor. I called your name, but you were gone."

I have been in the presence of death many times. I know what grief looks like. Survivors go through despair, anger, and even relief. What I sensed in Darcy was something entirely new. Anger sparkled darkly in her eyes, but she felt no grief. There was euphoria and a grudging disappointment . . . in me.

"Can I get you water or something?" I asked, needing a moment to process. I got up and went to the coffee stand. "I didn't kill your uncle, Darcy." I lied with my back to her.

"I know," she chuckled. "He isn't dead. He lost his arm from the blow. The worst of it is they think he's lost his mind. He keeps babbling about seeing the Grim Reaper. They put him in the crazy ward at the hospital. I think he's going to be there for a long time." She folded her hands in her lap and smirked at me. "What I want from you is money so I can take over my uncle's business. I can make it work. I'll be even better at it than he was, don't you agree? You always said I have all this promise."

"You're not a drug dealer, Darcy," I replied taking a drink of water. "And you're certainly not a pimp."

"And you're not a murderer, right?" She stood and walked to the door. "You know, I ought to thank you in way, Gwyn. I know how the world works now. Come by the bar tonight. I'll leave the door unlocked. I'll even fix you dinner. Be sure to leave a generous tip."

The news followed its predilection to ignore gang violence, and my plaz remained silent. I checked it frequently during the afternoon, finding no information regarding the uncle or new assignments. It occurred to me I may have been fired; if reapers could be fired. Who knew? Perhaps that was what Mr. Black had called to tell me. I decided not to return his call.

Instead, I called Betz. She pretended nothing had happened, not the murder and not the abrupt ending. Which was a shame because if I ever needed a conspiracy theory, it was then. Even a truly ridiculous one would have helped.

I left when Liz returned. I needed some fresh air to clear my head, and I set out, without really deciding to, to see if I could find the hospital where Uncle Tito had been taken. My plaz illuminated.

"Well, hello plaz! Long time no see." I pulled over to the side of the road, checked the GPS, and burst into laughter. It was directing me to the hospital to collect one Tito Mendez. Does it get more coincidental than that?

My relief was tangible. The tension in my neck melted away and the sense of dread I had been clinging to was suddenly gone. I felt like dancing or singing or just yelling "yahoo" at the top of my lungs. Fortunately, there was no one within hearing so I indulged myself with a shout.

Ten minutes later, the hospital loomed up in the distance like a giant concrete box. Five stories high with not a single architectural enhancement, the hospital emanated gloom. It might as well have had a neon sign flashing "abandon hope." I expected to see reapers lined up like Ubers in front of the entrance.

Visiting hours were in effect, so parking took a while. Long enough for me to wonder at the turn of events and kindle the hope things might right themselves. I took the elevator to the third floor, where Elly worked.

"Hey," I tapped her on the shoulder. She jumped up, surprised to see me standing there in my unhooded cloak.

"Oh, hi. Got an assignment?"

Her question was rhetorical, but I nodded anyway. "Where do you keep the crazies here?"

"Third floor. What's the name? I'll look up the room." Her hands played over the keys for a moment. "Room 316. But check your plaz, Gwyn. If it's an emergency like an MI, he may be in the ICU."

"I am the heart attack," I chuckled.

Elly blinked a few times before it registered. "Oh, you're here for the uncle. I didn't make the connection with the full name. But I didn't think the man's injuries were that serious."

"You never can tell," I replied. "I'm just glad he's on the way out. Pimps are despicable."

Elly shrugged. "I know. Only you've gotten too involved with this one. I knew you cared about the pretty waitress. But you should have just waited a few weeks for the system to take him out. Saved yourself the aggravation. You know what they say. The world is unfolding precisely as it should."

"Who says that?" I asked. "Besides billionaires and politicians." I had no doubt my actions had served to hasten the demise of a deplorable human. Lifting my hood, I made my way to room 316.

My assignment was lying quite alive in his bed, eyes glued to a ballgame on the TV. I stood at the foot of the bed and lowered my hood revealing the figure who had taken his arm. Tito sat up and shrieked. Grabbing at his chest, he tumbled from the bed to the floor. I could hear footsteps running in the hall. The monitors beside the bed began to beep alarmingly. I donned the hood and moved out of the way as the room filled with medical personnel. I waited until the man's heart stopped and his essence rose above the fray. Then I grabbed him by the throat and took him away.

The portal opened at our approach. One of the minions claimed Tito's soul and I watched them disappear into the dark region beyond. Tapping my plaz to conclude the assignment, I turned to leave.

"Come in, Gwendolyn," a familiar voice beckoned from the still-open portal.

After a moment's indecision, I passed through to the nether regions. Louie got the car door for me, and I climbed into the Bentley, noting the satisfied grin on my host's handsome face.

"How lovely to see you, my dear. When I learned of your arrival, I simply could not resist the opportunity to tell you how pleased I am this whole tawdry business is behind you. But there remains much we need to discuss."

Louis took us directly to the castle, leaving us at the immense stairway leading up to the massive edifice. Mr. Black said not a word but took my arm and led me into his home.

"It was you, wasn't it?" I asked in a voice barely audible as we walked to the dining room.

"Yes, it was I who kept you from making an egregious error. I was hopeful you would conclude why an intervention was necessary."

Mr. Black motioned to an elf who stood nearby. His name was George, and he scurried away to procure our food. He was adorable, three-foot-tall, with curly red hair parted on either side of his face revealing large, pointed ears. Just seeing him made me grin. He made several trips bringing salads, Cornish hens, asparagus, and slices of sausage I'd learned the elf made himself.

Mr. Black loved his cryptids. It was hard not to. The elves had a childlike charm and, like Louis, impeccable manners. George was only one of the elves employed at the castle. His fellows tended all the household chores within and without where a spectacular garden flourished in the constant night.

"Do you know why?" Mr. Black repeated his earlier question.

"Because murder, even the murder of a total dirtbag, is a crime?" I answered with my own question.

Mr. Black cut into his dinner. "It is, but that is not the reason. I care not about crime or punishment, for that matter. I intervened because of what such an action would do to you. In all the eons I have known you . . ."

"There you go again," I chided. "I have no memory of a past, much less one that includes you. If you are referring to reincarnation . . ."

"Technically, I am referring to reanimation. You are a reaper and thus not subject to reincarnation. A reaper either exists or does not exist. You are assembled from bits of matter and consciousness drawn from the infinite number of atoms floating in the universe."

"Assembled by whom, you? Is Hades Lord of the Universe?"

Mr. Black set aside his fork and sighed. "No, Gwyn, by the need for you. Need itself is creation. And once again, let me explain I am Mr. Black. I am one manifestation of the entity you call Hades, a supreme being who resides in yet another realm. There are others. Beelzebub, Lucifer, Satan, and the Devil are all personalities Hades can assume."

"Which one of them reassembled me?" I was not interested in Mr. Black's family tree. "It had to have been you."

He ran his fingers along his mustache. "No, my domain is at the other end of the process. I do not create. I disassemble. My minions reduce matter and consciousness to their basic form. Energy! They cleanse that which has failed to progress and release the rest into the void of space where it remains available to be reassembled into whatever form the universe requires."

He stood and led us into the living room and poured us each a snifter of brandy. "I see you are wearing the gift I gave you. Dare I interpret this as some measure of approval?"

I sighed. My head was spinning. "Do what you want."

He smiled. "I always do what I want."

Of that, I had no doubt. "And you wanted to bring me back."

He nodded his head. "I wanted that very much. Unfortunately, it was not my decision. Nor could I grant the forgiveness required."

Stunned, I sank into a chair. "Forgiveness for what?"

"Forgiveness for what you nearly did again." He poked the ashes in the fireplace and added a log to warm the large room.

My heart felt heavy. I was not merely a murderer. I was a serial killer, the worst kind of offender according to humans, "Well, damn. Who would have wanted to bring me back?"

"I for one." He confessed without hesitation. "You have always been especially dear to me, Gwyn. We were happy once. I wanted to be happy again."

I wanted to laugh. "Well, I guess that's not so surprising, the king of hell is into serial killers."

"Of course not. In all the eons I have known you, Gwyn; you were never a murderer. On the contrary, your act of rebellion was sparing someone. It was an act of kindness for a human who should never have survived. The act changed the order of things, the intended course of human evolution was disturbed. That cannot be permitted. The day you were reduced to atoms and cast into the solar wind was the worst moment of my long, long life."

He took me by the hand, then enfolded me in his arms. "A human poet said there is a place between good and evil. Let us see if we can find it again."

Louis drove me home the next morning. He told me he was surprised I had spent the night with Mr. Black. I smiled. Apparently, I was not the only perpetrator of incorrect assumptions.

"He loves you in so far as the master of the underworld is capable of love," Louis told me. "Never forget he is also complicated. One must look closely to see his motives."

Despite how my overnight visit may have appeared, Black and I had spent the time in conversation. Or possibly what could be called interrogation. I asked questions; Black evaded them. I got the gest of a relationship that had flourished off and on for eons. I also got the measure of a being whose manipulations knew no bounds.

"You should have stayed for breakfast," Louis continued the small talk. "The elves were creating a feast in celebration. Everyone is delighted to have you back.

"Except for me," I blurted out. "I have no memories of the previous me. No way to know the person being celebrated. I was a poser.

The Bentley pulled to the curb in front of my apartment. Louis escorted me to the door. He gave me a canine smile and kissed the back of my hand.

"I meant to thank you for the ancient tome, Louis," I whispered when he turned to leave.

He cocked his head to one side. "I recommend page 267."

Page 267 contained the final entry in the ancient tome. It was little more than a few paragraphs written in a firm, purposeful hand. The author had taken pains to form each letter as if the words encapsulated the crowning achievement of a life. It was written the year 1920.

"I have done what my thoughts required of me. The child is spared. I offer no apology. The life of a reaper

cannot weigh greater than the life of a human. I may have altered some small portion of human progression; and disturbed some grand plan. So be it. I readily accept the consequence.

"Hades is furious. His temper flashed like lightning day and night. He says I do not understand the future repercussions of what I have done. A reaper can never disobey a rule. Never decide who lives instead of dying. There is a hearing for my case. Hades will defend my indefensible actions. He will ask for leniency, but neither of us are optimistic. Louis told me my lover will ask that after I am destroyed when a sufficiency of time has passed, I will be reanimated save for any memory of what has happened. All knowledge of my life will be wiped away. Deeds, thoughts, and friends will never again be known to me.

"I am resolute against such an arrangement. How can those who punish me for disobedience disavow the rules themselves? I am a reaper meant to perform a function within the regulations assigned to me. I understand that I failed at my purpose and thus earned a punishment. To that end, I prefer a permanent oblivion.

"I shall leave these papers with gentle Louis. They are stories of the reapings that taught me most about humans and myself. He can bind the pages into a book if he chooses and keep it as a memento of me. A book is a perfect resting place for me as I have loved stories better than all other things."

It would have been a good time to have a friend with me. But I could not bring myself to put this burden on Elly or Betz, which left Felix to console me. He is not particularly good at that. He went to the kitchen and waited for his snack.

My hands shook as I prepared the mouse. I had just held my memories in my hand, thanks to Louis. I was the author of the many stories in the tome. Reading them gave me information, but it did not enable me to recall the details or relive the experience. The book might as well have told me I was Joan of Arc, for even if it had, I could not recall the heat of the fire. I put aside the book and closed my eyes; the past was known to me as fact alone. There was no richness or emotion as required for true remembrance.

What I do know is the world is not the small box in which I have kept myself since reawakening. There are luscious islands with soft, golden sand and tropical breezes. There are mountains that lift their snowy heads into the clouds. There are lakes so clear you can see pebbles on the bottom and stars enough to grant endless wishes.

I had been given a second chance by a system of which I do not approve; an elaborate cosmic mechanism where form and function substitute for purpose and will. I can try to be content. Felix is a master of self-satisfaction. But deep inside, I hear my voice urging me to find one of those beautiful places where with any luck, I might reap my own soul for once.

CHAPTER EIGHT

If You Want to Make Enemies, Try to Change Something

Betz had a new haircut. She looked like a porcupine with spikes of black hair protruding along the top of her head. I was glad we met at night when we could be alone without the need for our cloaks. A waning moon provided just enough light to see the fairies shimmering as they danced about the abandoned playground. I envied them their joy. Not much bigger than dragonflies, the ebullient little creatures flitted effortlessly through the cool night air. I could hear them singing an ancient song of thanks for the moon and the stars and the innocence of which they were made. The fairies fed on the energy left behind by the children who had played there in the day.

"Cute little buggers," Betz broke the silence we had settled into. "It is hard to believe fairies have existed for millions of years. They are so childlike."

"Maybe we should take notes," I sighed. "Reapers never have a childhood. We spring forth full grown like Athena from Zeus' head."

Betz slowly swiveled to face me. "She didn't have a childhood either?"

"Nope."

"Damn, maybe that's why humans are so weird. Childhood is a bitch; I mean, a kid is too small to do anything. And no one listens to them."

I pushed her shoulder and watched her head bounce like a frightened hedgehog. "What is up with your hair, Betz?"

"I'm incognito. Police are still looking for perps who attacked Darcy's uncle. I do not want to draw attention in case we were observed that night."

Even the fairies laughed. Everything about Betz' new look screamed for attention. The neon hot pants matched to a sleeveless purple vest, and boots that nearly burned my eyes. I tried to remember Betz's latest day job. She had said something about being an entertainer, if I recall correctly. A singer, or a magician's assistant, or a shaman for a new-age cult. Whichever, it had definitely bled over into her reaper life. It was the shock of Betz' non-conformity that made our friendship work. I considered asking her to join me on my contemplated vacation.

"Which reminds me," she said, taking a vial from her pocket. She poured a bit of liquid onto her fingers and reach up to smear the substance on my cheek. "There."

"Hey! What the fuck are you doing?" I yelled.

"Now you are blooded, you know, celebrating your first kill."

I checked my pockets for a tissue. "Get it off me, it stinks."

Betz put away the vial and made an effort to undo what she had done. "A guy told me this is what they always do when they go hunting. They honor the guy who got the kill by rubbing blood from the dead animal on his face."

"That better not be actual blood from Tito." I could not find anything to clean my forehead. "I mean it, Betz. Get it off me."

She lifted the hem of her shirt and tried to clean my face. "It is real blood. Not Tito's since I was not there in the hospital when you got him. "I filled the vial at a reaping earlier. I hope that doesn't invalidate the ritual. It was the best I could do." She inspected my cheek. "Shit, Gwyn, it doesn't want to come off. Want me to check the trash can for a wet diaper or something?"

I was considering asking the fairies for help, but the blood donor might have kicked the bucket because of COVID, leprosy, or low blood sugar, and I did not want to endanger them. The sprinklers came on twenty minutes later, which served to solve the problem.

I rinsed my face and filled my friend in about my visit with Mr. Black. I got a returned punch on the shoulder as a reward.

"All right, Gwyn. It's about time you started enjoying the perks of reaperhood. We get to enjoy human vices with none of the consequences. Well, as long we stay within two lines. No interference and no revealing who we are. All the rest is gravy."

I watched the fairies singing in the artificial rain and sighed. "You may be right. I have given some thought to taking a vacation."

"Oh my god! You just told me you found out you had a previous life, have been given a second chance, and the greatest-looking guy on the planet wants to have sex with you. And all you can say is you need a vacation." Betz nearly jumped off the bench we were sitting on. "From what? It's time you let yourself experience the good life."

"Are you forgetting about the coming Armageddon?" I smirked.

"No, but what can I do about that? Look, Gwyn, we are surrounded by death. It can consume us at times. The only way to deal with it is to try every good thing you can. Balance it out. Me? I take my moments where I find them. Like now."

She put her arm around my waist and pulled me closer. Her lips brushed mine gently for a moment then we were locked in a full-blown kiss. Staring cross-eyed at each other, we held our breath and waited for something warm to kindle in the gut. Or some urgent craving to speed the pulse. What we got was nothing whatsoever akin to passion.

When we parted, our eyes were locked in astonishment, though for different reasons. There had been no magic, no heat, no anything in the encounter.

Betz stood up and paced in a circle. "Damn girl, you are locked in neutral." She tossed her hands in the air. "I always get a better reaction than that. Did they leave out a few pieces when you got reassembled?"

"I did not get a manifest," I replied. Poets describe passion with lyrics about flushed body parts and an ache in the soul that must be satisfied. Whatever mechanism triggers those reactions had failed to engage in me.

Betz recovered in a few moments. "Blacky's got his work cut out for him if you ask me. So, on to Plan B. You need to find another activity that appeals to you. You don't drink; you obviously aren't a partier or a fan of drugs—not that drugs have any real effect on us. Other than the occasional attempt at murder, what the hell do you do for fun, Gwyn?"

The sprinklers turned off, and the fairies stopped their dancing to listen to my answer.

"I don't remember. Remember?" I pointed out defensively, adding, "I like to read."

Even the fairies groaned. The ground quivered and bucked beneath us. Trees swayed ominously, and a jolt nearly knocked me off the bench. The quake was much stronger than previous temblors. It lasted long enough to portend damage, and we could hear the sirens beginning their sad yodels. Our plazzes went off, and we ran to our cars.

Dear Felix. He is always happy to see me when I get home, and he has no opinion on what kind of reaper I should become. Although if I decided to become simply content like he is, I don't think he would be disappointed. Of course, both of us knew that was not going to happen.

A change of venue kept licking at my mind. The best I could do, given the uncertainties of the times, was to renovate my personal space. I took down the Grim Reaper posters, packed up those books which I knew I would not read, and ordered new linens from Amazon. Felix defended his cage, evidently happy with the status quo.

I selected sage green for the living room and a pretty blue for the bedroom and had the hardware store deliver paint and the paraphernalia to put it on the walls. I rewarded my hard work by splurging on ice cream and cigarettes, neither of which were especially satisfying. So, I ordered delivery from an Italian place Liz had recommended. By Thursday afternoon, I had a new crib and a closet filled with colorful garments totally unsuitable for the office. Liz was going to freak.

All this was accomplished between half a dozen reapings. The most notable involved a pair of idiots who had broken into a fireworks factory to smoke drugs and blown themselves to pieces. I made a note that when a human body is shredded, the soul rises intact from the largest piece. Saves a lot of soul searching, I told Felix, who side-eyed me and retreated to his cage.

I limited my forays for the week to trips to my office and back. Souls wandered the suburbs because reapers often found it impossible to locate a portal ready to receive them. They were invisible to even the most sensitive of humans. But even unseen, the presence of the newly dead laid a general malaise on the environment. Something was wrong; everyone could feel it, and no one knew what was causing it. If one listened, you could hear the wheels coming off the universe.

Elly sounded intrigued when I told her Tito's had reopened under Darcy's management. We agreed to meet for lunch to check the place out. I had given Darcy the money she wanted, and she had spent it well. The place was painted a subtle grayish rose, which matched the new furniture and made the place seem larger.

There were two waiters, a young dark-haired woman who could have been Darcy's mini-me. And an even younger boy who rushed about serving customers who mainly wanted to be left alone. The bartender had returned, but as far as I could tell, he and the name Tito's Pub were all that remained of the original eatery.

Elly left a message she might be late due to an assignment. I took a table at the back of the room and ordered a Guinness and two prime rib platters from the new plasticized menu. I asked the waitress to hold the food back until my guest arrived. Elly appeared ten minutes later and eyed the new décor with an approving smile.

"Nice," she commented, taking the chair opposite me. "Your little friend, Darcy, has taste, I see. It appears your venture into criminality has yielded the result you hoped for."

"Hum-mmmm, anything's possible," I said as our dinners were delivered.

Elly ordered a Dos Equis® and inspected the cut of meat she had been given. "Still harboring some guilt, Gwyn? That is a waste of time. Besides, this looks nearly perfect. Take pride in having improved the food. It is not the best prime rib on Earth. But it is lovely."

She took a bite and smiled happily.

"You've had prime rib everywhere on Earth?" I asked.

Elly huffed. "More countries than you could ever possibly imagine, Newbie."

"I cannot imagine very many countries that serve prime rib, Elly. And it is time to stop thinking of me as a newbie. I have earned my stripes."

"He got to you!" she gloated. "I warned you he would. Now that you know about the relationship the two of you had, he will demand more. And if you disappoint him, he will never call."

"He already did. He left roses in my apartment while I was out on a reap."

"What color?" she demanded, her eyes twinkling with anticipation.

I grinned. "Black roses!"

Elly made a tent with her fingers. "You don't say. You have no idea what he went through to get you back. What it cost him. I sincerely hope you don't make Mr. Black regret what he's done." She turned her attention to the dinner giving me time to assess what she was telling me. "You must have something special under all that rebelliousness."

I accepted the characterization as a compliment. On the other hand, Elly was less than complimentary about my recent behavior.

"You carried things too far again, Gwyn. And not in a nice way. When I knew you back then, you wanted to save everyone. Now, you are acting like a vigilante. It is not a good look. I volunteered to mentor you when I learned you were being reassembled. Thought we could get you off to a grand start, bring out your better angels, and speed you up the ladder." She wiped her mouth with the napkin and sighed. "You will not get a third chance, Gwyn. Accept the straight and narrow. A reaper is a simple being. Read your books, follow your plaz, and make Mr. Black happy for as long as he remains fond of you. Which reminds me, is it true the werewolf, what's his name, Louis, gave you a book?"

"Yes," I said, wondering how Elly had divined that particular detail.

"I remember how you used to like to write stories. I don't suppose your stories managed to find their way into the book, did they? I doubt Mr. Bla . . ."

"Mr. Black asked you to find out," I voiced my assumption. This one seemed a better chance of being accurate, at least considering the blush spreading across Elly's face.

"Mr. Black is not a trusting individual," she took an off-ramp. "He's been betrayed many times. Of course, he is not above a good backstabbing in his own right."

It was hard not to feel concern for Louis. Despite his appearance, he was one of the most gentle and honorable beings I knew. I took a bite of salad and decided to move the conversation in yet another direction.

"Do you think the earthquakes are a prelude to the event we are expecting?"

"That would be lovely," Elly smiled. "But I fear there is worse than that to come. Thinking back on events like Pompeii, Lisbon, Antioch, and other catastrophes, hundreds of thousands of humans can be killed in the twinkling of an eye. I think that's what Mr. Black is trying to upgrade his processors for." She asked the waitress to bring our dessert and coffee. "My personal suspicion is an event, like a meteor. It's been eons since the planet has experienced one of those."

As Elly and I were leaving, the police burst into Tito's and arrested Darcy. Even the best plans can come to a disappointing conclusion, I thought, watching Darcy perp walked to the cruiser. Betz wanted me to be more hedonistic. Elly wanted me to become more obedient. Mr. Black wanted me to . . . something. I had no idea what I wanted, but it would no longer involve liberating Darcy or anyone else. The thought of all those changes only made me angry.

"Did you see the video of that volcano?" Liz asked when I returned to the office. She was at her desk, her attention directed at the screen in front of her. "My goodness, those poor people in Iceland."

I had no idea what people she was referring to. The eruption was not the horror that had occurred historically in Indonesia. Or even a fraction of the damage events like Mount Vesuvius had delivered to Pompei. Icelandic volcanoes numbered over a hundred and go off regularly without killing anybody. Grímsvötn, Katla, Snaeflilsness—the greatest danger they presented was tongue-tying newscasters. This eruption would be less debilitating; Helka was easier to pronounce.

I leaned over her desk and got a look at the video engrossing Liz. My first thought was how beautiful the eruptions were. Channels of red lava were running down the flanks of white mountains. Behind them, steely gray smoke surged into a darkened blue sky laced with green aurora borealis trails.

Leaving my assistant to her video obsession, I went into my office. If volcanic activity were to cause the end of the world, doomsday would at least be colorful. In my mind, I did not sense some impending tragedy. Humans were progressing, albeit in fits and starts. I had been reassembled, an outcome for which Mr. Black had evidently paid a considerable price. There was more evidence things would continue in a world already fraught with hardship. I put aside any consideration that the end of days had begun, which was more than Liz was willing to do.

Liz came into my office with files in one hand and the remains of a giant chocolate bar in the other.

"They've shut down air traffic over Europe because of the volcano." Liz sounded positively enthusiastic about the news. "Do you think this is it?

"IT?" I queried.

Liz huffed. "The Rapture! All the good people go to heaven, and the rest of us stay here to eke out an existence. Until we reach perfection."

Now, that would be one hell of an evolution for humans, I thought, but said, "You are a good person, Liz. If this is the rapture, I'll miss you." I found it impossible to hide the sarcasm.

Liz looked distressed. "You are a good person too. But it is not likely working for the IRS is a ticket to heaven. It says that about tax collectors in the Bible. Maybe we should relocate to some safe place like Alaska."

The illogic of my assistant's proclamations was always a high point of my day, and I made a mental note that the rapture was not expected in Alaska. Even so, relocating is not a reaper's choice. According to Mr. Black, the system sends reapers where it wills. Our "day jobs" are ours to select. The rest is programmed. The plaz lights up with a notification, and a plane or train ticket arrives via courier. Thirty-six hours later, our belongings are donated, bank accounts are closed, and we are ensconced in a new place. I know of only one such relocation to have occurred in the current times, and that is only via rumor.

The evening sky was an eerie color. Clouds were tinged in a rusty gray, and behind them the darkening sky was studded with pastel splotches. There was a charge in the air and evidence the underworld had not corrected the portal problem. I saw several newly deads lurking beneath an overpass, but my plaz did not light, so I left them to the assigned reapers.

Felix was agitated when I arrived home. He slithered from room to room, looking for a place to feel safe. He ignored the mouse I offered and curled under the sofa. I sat in the side chair and pulled my legs up in my personal rendition of a coil. My cell phone rang. Seeing it was Liz, I put it on speaker, thinking Felix might enjoy listening.

"Oh, Gwyn. Thank heaven you are safe," Liz said. "Do you have any idea what is going on?"

"I usually get my updates from you," I told her.

"Then you haven't seen it," Liz shrieked. "The sky is turning black and strange lights are appearing."

"I think that's called night, and those would be stars," I chuckled. The image of Liz wearing a tin foil hat filled my mind's eye.

"Not these." She insisted. "These are fiery bits coming out of the firmament right through the clouds."

"Calm down, Liz. There is an old saying—red skies at night, sailors delight. Only in this case, I think you probably saw a meteor shower."

"Or angels come to activate the rapture."

"If that proves accurate, give them my regards."

My plaz was filled with weird lines and flashing symbols. I took the phone with me to the window and looked down at the street. There were dozens of newly dead strolling sidewalks where the living could neither hear nor see them. A cop was directing traffic at an intersection, and the dead were mimicking his hand movements like a spectral chorus line. Every now and then, a car would pass through a spirit who would shake its fist at the vehicle.

"I'm sure it's nothing to fret about, Liz. "But you can take tomorrow off if you want to." She thanked me and told me to stay safe before hanging up.

Okay, you don't have to hit me in the head with a gravestone before I get it. Something was up. More than uncooperative portals or a glitch in the system. Doubting I could reach Elly, I opened the ancient tome, hoping to find an event that was similar to what was happening. To my surprise, I did. I settled on the sofa, tapping it to entice Felix to join me. There was a single paragraph that raised the hair on my arms.

"The firmament has been parted once again. The dead have risen and haunt the Earth in numbers too great to manage. I have taken refuge in the cathedral among hundreds of terrified humans who debate the cause of what is happening. They fear the Age of Noah has returned. Or the wrath of the gods is being visited upon them for their wickedness. Some speak

of demons, for the very ground beneath us lurches and falls open. Much may be destroyed, but all will begin again!"

All will begin again! My mind had a moment of clarity into which insight leaped. Damn, Felix. I think Atlantis and Göbekli Tepe just got explained. Evidently, when humans screw up, a cosmic repair service is dispatched to perform a clean-up on aisle Earth.

I nudged my reading buddy and got a tongue flicker in response. It was his version of a high five. I understood at a deeper level why I had written the stories in the book so long ago. Even then, I had wanted to fathom the purpose of my existence and the system which I served. I picked up a pen and made a few new entries on the blank sheets of parchment at the back of the tome. I started with the story of Millie Maise.

The storm outside intensified; gusts of wind rattled the window and threatened the integrity of our building. I sank back on the sofa and closed my eyes to ponder what events might happen before everything changes and all begins again.

CHAPTER NINE

All of Our Journeys Are in the Mind

When I opened my eyes again, I was standing at a window, watching trails of moonlight ripple on a tranquil sea. Where there had been chaos, there was serenity and the comfort of a familiar presence.

I turned from the window and learned I was in a small octangular room festooned with nautical appointments. The walls were cluttered with ropes and netting. There was a table with chairs, a cabinet with equipment for measuring wave and weather, a chifforobe, and a bed.

"Why have you brought us to a lighthouse?" I my asked my companion.

"Not just a lighthouse, Gwyn. We are in the Watch Room of the Lighthouse of La Jument on Ushant Island in Western Brittany." Mr. Black opened a picnic basket and spread a checkered cloth across a table as he spoke. "You have been dreaming about a vacation. I thought I might oblige."

He smoothed the cloth and began placing containers of food from a basket neatly on the table, slowly revealing a feast.

"Let me rephrase the question," I smiled as I inspected each of the exotic dishes displayed in front of me. "Um, *why* are we in here?"

Mr. Black offered me a chair and then sat beside me. We tapped our glasses, which were filled with a delicious golden liquid new to my palette. We piled our plates with succulent bits, each more tantalizing than the next.

"We are here for the storm." He finally told me.

We were forty meters above the surface of a sea known for its violent weather. I had seen the picture of the giant waves enclosing the structure. I gave him a quizzical look. The ocean showed not the slightest agitation; the brewing cataclysm had been left far behind.

"There is not a cloud in the sky," I pointed out.

Mr. Black set down his silver fork and met my eyes with his. "It is a metaphor, Gwyn, for the quandary in which we find ourselves. You are here with me, because despite your penchant for breaking the rules, I wish you to be. And I assure you a storm is coming. A storm unlike any you might imagine."

I could imagine quite a lot, especially the devastation I assumed was happening to my friends. "Please tell me you are not the author of all this."

"I am not the reason for the storm, my dear," He wiped his napkin across his mouth. "You are."

A slap across the face would have shocked me less. "That is impossible!" I shot back, getting to my feet and walking away. I knew what he was referring to. Old sins cast long shadows. "This is about that child I saved, isn't it?"

"Gwyn, darling. None of that matters any longer." He assured me, using that smooth seductive tone like a cattle prod to move my thoughts elsewhere.

Charm wasn't going to work this time and I moved to the window and watched clouds moving in, erasing the stars and making the night sky even darker. This was no longer my personal sad little story. I had made a mistake and got my ass kicked into a billion pieces. But what was happening outside involved the whole damn world.

"It matters more than ever," I told him. "I need to understand why. Without my memory, the idea I saved a child is no different to me than the stories in that ancient book."

"Ah, yes, the tome Louie returned to you." Mr. Black joined me at the window. "Unfortunate of him to do that. I wanted us to start anew."

"I've read the stories over and over trying to recreate the me I once was." Rain began to fall and the temperature even in the room chilled.

Mr. Black paced for a time. The storm seemed to grow stronger with each step he took. The lighthouse groaned as waves began to mount the foundation. I watched the rain claw at the window.

"So, this is how the universe punishes disobedience?"

Mr. Black laughed. "This is not a punishment, Gwyn, it is a correction. Humanity is being returned to its original course."

"Okay, even if this storm is supposed to correct a mistake, I deserve to know who the child was." I had to know. If we were talking Hitler or any of the other tyrants from history, I needed to deal with it. "When . . . how did it happen? You owe me that much?"

"His name is unimportant." Mr. Black began packing the remains of our supper. "He was the son of an ordinary family. He was bright and inquisitive, a budding genius for which humanity is not yet ready. He must have gotten a modicum of Eistein's consciousness while forming in the womb."

That can happen? Mr. Black chuckled. "It's not common, Gwyn. I told you nothing is lost in the universe. The random selection of molecules keeps things interesting.

"The boy was slated to die along with several other children when a truck crashed into his preschool classroom. You were assigned to the reaping. When you arrived, two of the children were already dead. The boy, however, clung to life. You touched him and felt his fear. He wanted to live and you could not bring yourself to let him die."

"Did I know this kid?"

"Personally? No." Mr. Black shook his head. "But there is an amusing connection. Your current office assistant was his older sister. It happened forty-seven years ago. Liz never got over the trauma the accident caused her family."

That accounted for Liz's fascination with disasters, I mused. Her snacking fetish remains unexplained.

"Because you saved the boy, he grew to manhood and became a brilliant computer analyst. His algorithms are thrusting technology into a future the human psyche is not yet evolved to manage. AI is his forte."

"Wait, wait, wait. Why not just eliminate the guy?" I interrupted. "This storm is tossing mankind back to the Middle Ages? A little extreme, don't you think?"

"No, no. The system has been unreliable. Eliminating a single human might not be successful. He's already made discoveries." Mr. Black tossed his hands in the air. "You are not capable of understanding these matters. It's more like the 1900s, not the Middle Ages. One must be extremely careful about the timeline." He sounded irritated to be challenged. "It is true that a few million or perhaps a billion humans will probably die in the aftermath. Reapers will have their hands full like I've been warning you. But humans will be returned to the proper evolutionary course. The planet itself will heal from humanity's bungling."

I did not believe him. Who gave Mr. Black the right to manipulate humanity, I wondered. He ran the underworld, the gigantic recycling bin that converted human minds into energy. I was seeing Mr. Black for the egotist Elly had described. "Why did you bring me back? The real reason, please."

He responded with a maniacal grin. "I want you back. You are unique. Your penchant to question rules makes you all the more sexy. And you actually loved me once. You have no idea how rare that is, Gwyn. What you did by saving that child gave me the justification for this storm. Technology makes humans much too powerful, too competent about solving the little roadblocks I enjoy placing in their way." The grin turned evil as he spoke. "After all, I am a demon, Gwyn. You should know me by now."

"Know you?" I shouted above the storm. "I don't even know your full name."

"My given name is Nilo. It means judgment." He replied in a soft voice, moving closer to take me in his arms. "We are created to be precisely what we are."

"Nilo suits you." I felt his charisma pulling me in.

He caressed my hair, and I wanted to melt into him, but the storm was tearing at my soul.

"There is something you can do to repair the damage," he whispered in my ear. You can calm my fury by being mine once again and we can be as we once were."

I could feel deep within myself that Nilo was wrong. I am not who I was. Saving a single child had altered human evolution. One could hardly divine what saving the whole world would do. Whatever "all begins again" means, it cannot mean just that.

Sensing my hesitation, Black released me. He settled into a chair and poured himself a glass of wine.

"No," I said turning away rather than watch his reaction.

Nilo cursed and rose to his feet. "I assure you I have told you the truth. Just look."

He snapped his fingers, and a door opened in my mind. A single memory slipped through. I was holding a child's broken body in my arms. A voice was screaming "No, no!" And I was sobbing.

I turned to find Nilo sneering at me. His face was an ancient mask of fury. The demon had revealed more than a single memory. He had revealed his true self. It was not my rebellion that had been the problem. It was the fact a mere human child had experienced an act of kindness, Nilo knew he himself never would.

The storm screamed at us, shattering the window and letting the ocean burst in.

What was left of my apartment was minimal. I found Felix's body in what had been our bedroom and buried him at the foot of a rock pile where I imagined mice liked to scurry. I marked the grave with a page from the ancient tome. The story of Bigotes and a reptiles's revenge.

I packed up my reaper tools and headed out of the destroyed city dressed in dungarees and my cloak. There were bodies evident from time to time: humans and other species. All had fallen to the storm. Even the land bore witness to the violence, as if a reaper's scythe had gouged and sheared it.

There were no spirits to be seen. Either reapers had worked through the storm, which I found unlikely, or Mr. Black's minions had indeed lent a hand. The living were gathered in groups, foraging for food and constructing shelters. What had to be a consuming grief was kept at bay by the work of staying alive.

I came upon an elderly man struggling to lift a heavy wooden sign blocking the entrance to a damaged church. Together, we managed to turn the sign over and read the signage still partly there.

HE END IS NEA

"Hard to disagree with that," the man remarked. "Guess I should have listened to the priest. Never saw a thunderstorm that mean in all my life. I hid out in my bunker yonder. I was thinking the government was going to come get us one day. Never expected this kind of thing. My bunker's dug back twenty yards. I sat in there listening to the sound of the world dying."

I nodded. "Hard to anticipate a storm that big."

"I wonder what made the padre put up that particular message. The end was near all right. Padre's body is over there. Guess he didn't take himself seriously enough. I always wondered if religious fanatics believe the scary stuff they say."

"Might have been a lucky guess," I replied, shouldering my backpack.

"Ain't much lucky about it," the man said, giving me a wave as I left.

"Question is, who made the devil do this?" a disembodied voice muttered as I made my way down the road. It was the priest, Father Ryna, who drifted up and introduced himself. His body was a twisted mass in a nearby tree. I offered to take him to the portal if we could find one.

"No thanks, I know the way. I was just waiting for the rush to be over. A bunch of little guys came running and led the souls that way." He pointed to the woods.

Must have been the elves, I thought. The fairies were busy picking through the bits of flora scattered everywhere. I could hear them swearing in voices that sounded like foul-mouthed children. Ryna could also see them.

"Are those the new masters of the planet?" He asked.

"Nope. They've been here as long as humans have," I told him. "You just never believed in anything but the specialness of your own existence."

"Believing was my job description." The priest frowned. "I think my soul needed glasses."

The damage was severe but survivable, as witnessed by the bands of humans who were working together to forage for food and removing debris. I came across merely a dozen or so newly dead. They occupied themselves picking through the rubble of what had been homes and vehicles. None took me up on my offer to lead them to the portal. My plaz was not working. Feeling no urgency to insist they come with me, I left them to their dawdling.

Portal stones were scattered about the ground, intermixed with the remains of trees that had been carried for miles by the wind. Light from the setting sun cast shades of red and yellow on the scene. I paused to enjoy the beauty of it. I saw reapers roaming about the entrance. Most had never entered past the portal and were debating if they should go inside. I strolled through the opening, and they followed happily when I wasn't immediately vaporized.

Inside, the underworld appeared untouched by the storm. The landscape was a meticulous as usual, capped by a deep blue sky where the sun had yet to set. Mr. Black could set the environment to any time of day or night he wished. Evidently, he wanted the greatest contrast possible with the devastated human realm.

Betz spotted me on the road to Mr. Black's castle.

"Where have you been, girl," she asked, grabbing me into a crushing hug. "You didn't bring that snake of yours, did you?"

"He's dead."

Betz grimaced. "Sorry. But dead is definitely the word of the day."

There was no doubt of that. There was no way to count the victims of the storm, only a need to return the terrible harvest to the ground.

Elly was sitting with several reapers at a gazebo midway between the castle and one of the expansive gardens. Betz and I decided to join them.

"There she is!" Elly waved in greeting. "We were just trying to figure out where you might be. Mr. Black has not been seen yet, either. So, you cannot fault my friends here for their lusty suspicions," she grinned.

"He's not here?" I had assumed Nilo had returned to his castle.

"No one's there but the wolf man," Betz clarified. "Unless you count the house elves. And they are all dead tired."

Elly studied my reaction while I replied to greetings from the other reapers and sat down next to her. "Mr. Black didn't tell you where he was going, did he?" she whispered.

"No. I thought he would be here."

"We thought you would know," Elly admitted. "When the portals collapsed, we kept waiting for Mr. Black to do something. We think the powers that be were none too pleased with what Mr. Black was doing. The storm suddenly just stopped. One minute it was the mother of all hurricanes. The next it was clear blue sky."

Betz pointed to the sky. "Now, he sleeps with the fishes," she said in a mocking mob accent. We all groaned. "Hey, Pisces is a fish. If you ask me, Mr. Black's bits belong out there."

That spurred outright laughter. Elly put her hand on my shoulder. "What Betz means is . . ."

"I know what she means," I stopped her. "Nothing is lost. Certainly not my heart." I looked up at the cosmos. Somewhere, in the vast cold of space, Nilo's essence chafed amid the stars. I could live with that. Although I had the feeling Nilo was not completely gone and probably would be back. After all, it had happened to me.

"I cannot believe I slept with him," Betz sighed.

"I can." Elly laughed. "The way I hear it . . ."

"Hey!" Betz bristled. "The way I heard it, you were Black's bed partner a time or two. The guy was charming when he wanted to be."

Several of the reapers nodded affirmatively. "You would not want to see him when he wasn't," I had to add.

Betz sat down beside me. "I could use a cappuccino. How about you?"

"You'll have to wait a while. Starbucks has no electricity." One of the reapers pointed out. "A four hundred-mile-an-hour wind demolished all the power stations. Took out technology firms completely. I heard the target was the whole internet infrastructure. Computers, cell phones—anything that uses electricity are just gone."

"What are humans supposed to do?" a reaper asked. "Cook squirrels over wood chips for dinner?"

"That won't work," Betz chuckled. "There aren't that many squirrels left at the moment."

I hadn't thought of that. The correction was more than the loss of GTA or FB. Access to information had been interrupted. Leaving humanity to use its wits instead of staring at a screen to learn how to solve a problem.

"They are doomed," Elly mused aloud.

"I do not agree with that assumption, folks." Louis' rich, baritone voice carried across the lawn as he approached. He was escorting a girl aged six or seven. Her left arm was in a sling and her right hand held an ice cream bar she was happily devouring.

Turns out the mild-mannered werewolf was more than a chauffeur. He was the guy behind the scenes who kept the place humming. It was Louis who handled operations, kept the books honest, and had a back channel to other realms. Mr. Black had been the face of the underworld; Louis was the heart. When Mr. Black decided to reassemble me and send humanity back to an electronic dark age, Louis arranged to mitigate the damage. He returned my memories by giving me the tome and kept an eye on my interactions with Nilo.

"I'll be damned," I said to no one in particular.

"Unlikely," Louis shook his head and handed the girl to Elly. "Hell is completely full, and I have need of every reaper."

Louis stepped into the center of the gazebo. The new CEO cut a remarkable figure, dressed in a suit and tie with a Panama hat raked over his ears.

"Human civilization will continue," He assured us. "They have survived worse in the past. The physical infrastructure may be gone, but the knowledge to recreate it remains. We secured the best of their leaders and scientists before the storm began. Each of you played a role in that effort, and I thank you. Humanity thanks you. Now, I am sure you must have concerns about how we proceed."

Elly spoke first. "Our plaz devices are not functioning."

Louis nodded. "We're working on that. In the meantime, use your instincts. You'll find you have a talent you never imagined."

"You said humans will survive. How? They need food and shelter."

"Help them procure it. It is perfectly okay to share your knowledge and physical strength. The fairies and elves are excellent resources."

"What about our needs?" Betz called out. "I just want a cappuccino."

Louis shook his head. "The grid should be restored within a year, Betz. Meanwhile, we will be up and running in a few days. I'll keep a pot of coffee ready for you."

Drake raised his hand. "The strong are going to prey on the weak."

Louis nodded thoughtfully. "They always have, but you do not have to permit that. You can, should even, do what is necessary to remove a menace."

"You mean we can kill humans?" Elly sounded horrified at the idea. "I am not really into that judgment thing."

"Then you are not a reaper," Louis pressed the point. "Sympathy is not for the wicked, it is for the innocent. Saving them is an act of kindness." He looked at me. "You understand, don't you Gwyn."

I did, indeed.

The air beside Louis shimmered as a womanly form appeared. She was the woman from the conference who had commanded such attention when she had summoned reapers for dinner. She was incredible looking. The bloom of youth had given way to the radiance of wisdom. The pearl-gray gown she wore gathered at her shoulders, giving the impression of folded wings.

"Holy shit! Angels are real?" Betz whispered.

Louis smiled. "She is a Guardian."

The woman enlightened us with a description of a new order in which each life form fulfills a necessary function. As I listened, it became apparent I was meant to save the child. I am a reaper but my actions are not preordained. My decisions are measured as good or evil, like all other beings.

The most significant victim of the storm had been the system itself. There were errors and glitches aplenty. Mistakes were made and would need to be corrected. Mr. Black was gone, and with him, the old excuse: *the devil made me do it.*

Many humans have died, and many more will join them. Their bodies returned to the Earth. Their consciousness spread throughout the universe. Until a will greater than any we can comprehend, arises. And all begins again.

ABOUT THE AUTHOR

Mary Eicher lives in Southern California with her two daughters. With degrees in English Literature and Psychology, she left an executive position in Silicon Valley to pursue her love for writing. Mary has traveled extensively in Europe and worked with the Pacific Whale Foundation in Australia and dolphin research facilities in Hawaii. Recipient of numerous awards, including a Knight-Ridder Silver Pen Award and the Kops-Fetherling Gold Award for LGBTQ Fiction.

Email:	maryeic@aol.com
Website:	officialmaryeicher.com
Facebook:	www.facebook.com/mary.eicher.338
X (Twitter):	MaryEicher19

ADDITIONAL BOOKS BY MARY EICHER
The Artemis Series:
The Harbinger
Perceptions
Revelations
Temis and Lofn

www.ingramcontent.com/pod-product-compliance
Lightning Source LLC
Chambersburg PA
CBHW071437130726
47997CB00006B/2119